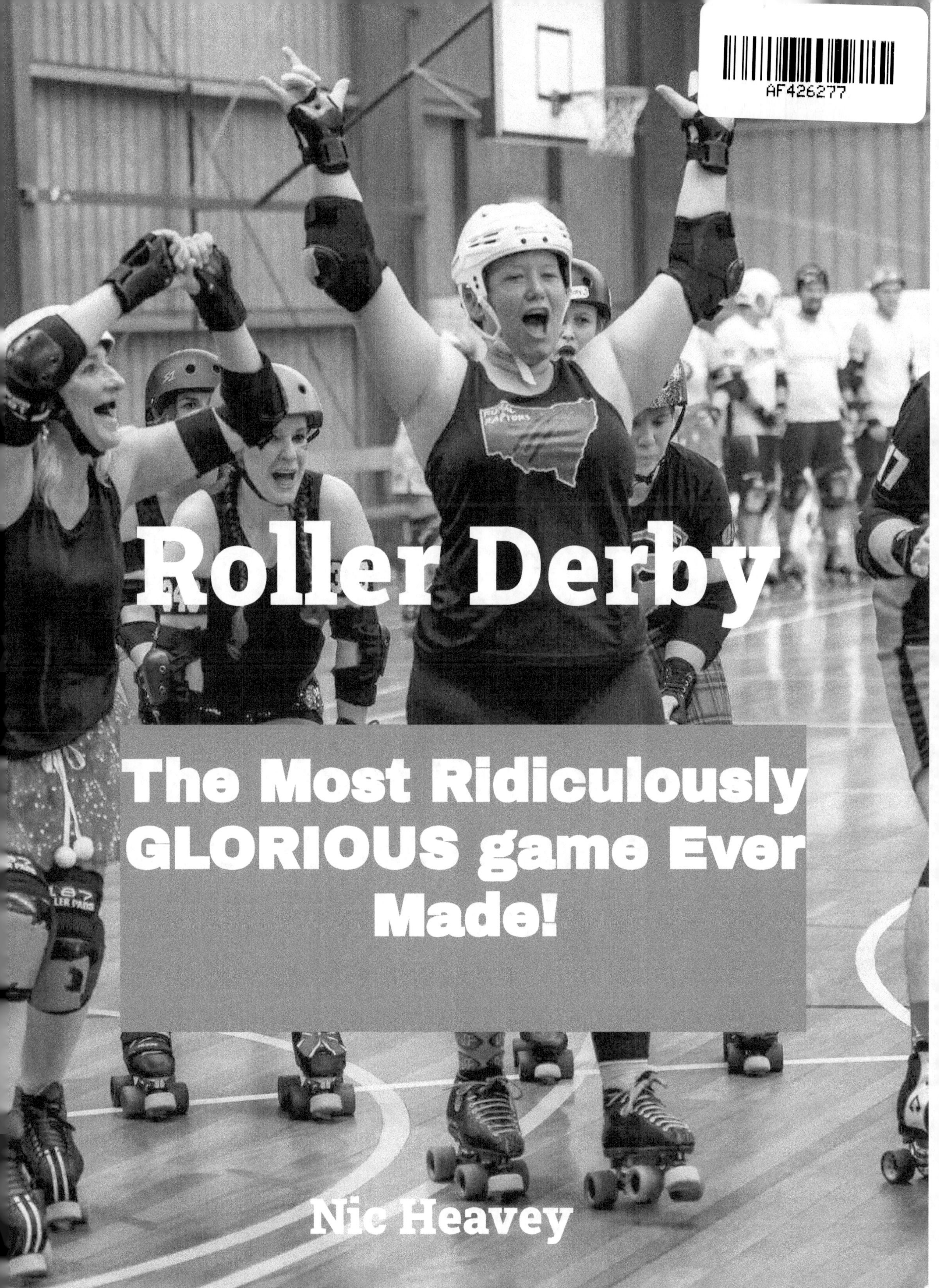

AF426277
Roller Derby
The Most Ridiculously GLORIOUS game Ever Made!
Nic Heavey

When someone asks........What is Roller Derby?

This has to be the most startling question I receive. I almost have a jaw dropping, I'm almost offended moment in which I must contain myself from dramatically overeacting at the audacity of others not knowing about my sport of choice.

What is roller Derby, you say?

Why my dear friend, let us pause a moment while I collectively take a deep breath and compose my sheer joy at what is about to change your view of life. (yes I am a little enthusiastic to get started) right.....deep breath.....

Roller Derby (while a young sport, it has an interesting history, but more on that later) is only the most ridiculously glorious game ever made!!

The absolute best Full bodied contact sport in existence!

(I dare you to argue with me :) Of course you cant because I will win this!)

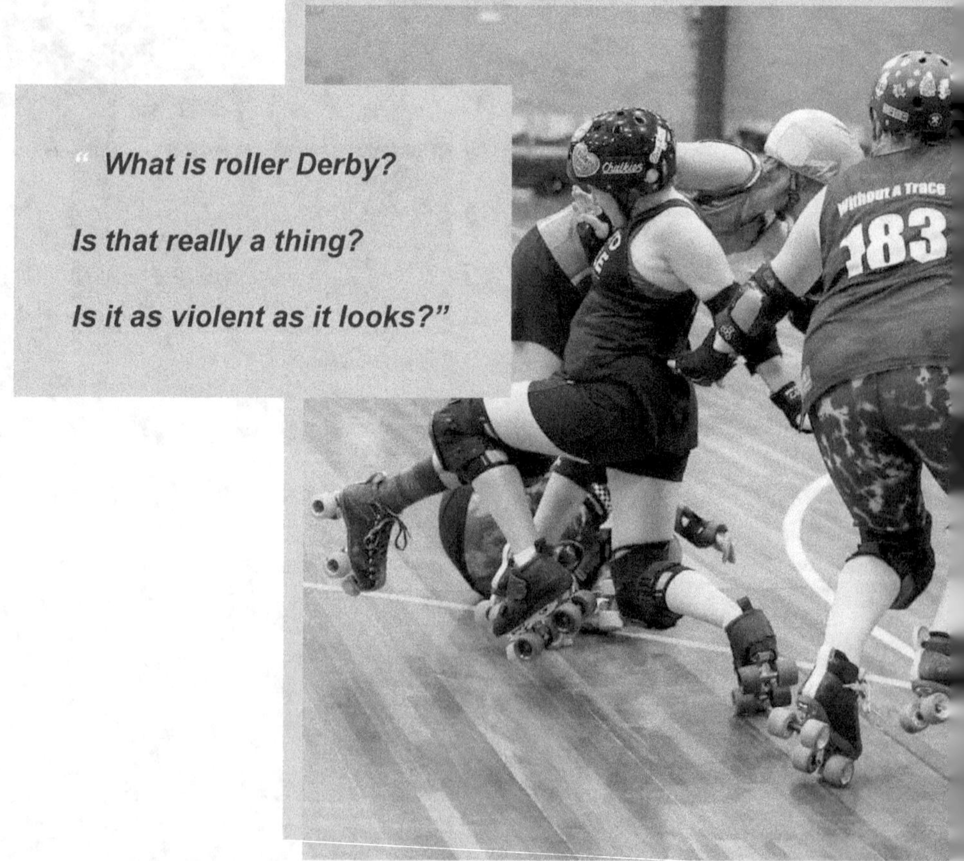

"What is roller Derby? Is that really a thing? Is it as violent as it looks?"

These are the general responses I get when I mention that I play Roller Derby to others.

While I try really hard not to eye roll (sometimes I fail in this) I generally am excited to respond, why this could be a new person to induct into the most epic and brilliant world of Roller Derby.

Ok, so in the words of Rika Havok….."hear me out"……. (epic ideas, thoughts and stories always begin with this sentence).

Roller Derby is a full bodied contact sport played on roller skates, yes it totally is a thing, and its just as violent as any other full bodied contact sport (think rugby or ice hockey).

It reminds me of a combination of a rugby league scrim because there is a lot of pulling and pushing.

Combine that with a game of Chess because of the strategy behind the game; and the sport is played both offensively and defensively; and a pinball machine, because if you do make impact there is a likely chance you will ricochet …… and then add wheels (roller skates) to this whole process.

This is usually where I would ask if I could draw a picture or rearrange a bunch of people to now become derby players to better visually explain the complexities of the Derby.

"Is there a ball?"

This question always makes me giggle and I usually respond "yeah, me" I'm like the pin ball, but no, no actual ball.

Welcome aboard the Derby Train (more commonly known as a pace line), I'm Nikki

(AKA Mu FasTa...... as in I always Nita MuFasTa) and I am so glad you are here.

If you are reading or listening to this book most likely you already play derby or you want to know more.....either way you have come to right place, for this book is about ALL THINGS ROLLER DERBY!

I cant wait to know y'all better and welcome you, athlete, hero, to a new world, otherwise known as the Derby Verse.

Today's Derby is rolled out (yes expect endless skatey puns) on a flat, oval shaped

(it's called an ellipses, hello) track with two opposing teams ready to display some mad athleticism and a terrifying battle of bodies all done on wheely boots otherwise known as roller skates.

This is Roller Derby.

A full bodied, 100% injury risk contact sport.

Roll out first please!!!

Have your roll out song ready!!!…….

Derby makes an entrance, we let you know we have arrived.

5 players on each team (10 on the track at one time) , 2 Jammers, 6 blockers, 2 pivots and a partridge in a pear tree, well no partridge or tree for that matter.

This is Roller Derby.

The Jammers (look for the helmets with the star   ) begin on the starting line and a time keeper blows a whistle and yells "5 seconds!" countdown......4....3.....2....1.....another whistle blows and the jammers then have to haul ass to get through the packs of bodies presented in front of them (some helping, some aiming to build walls that can feel like their made of solid brick) in a race to make it round the track, flat chat, only to do it all again and again and again for the honour of scoring points to gain the title of lead Jammer in this race of chaos and mayhem.

How does one earn the points?

You might ask.

Simple, by passing the opposing blockers hips of course. Or nowadays called the centre body mass.

This is why blockers create walls of "butts" and "braces" trapping Jammers in what has been dubbed 'the sad place' where ones soul goes to be crushed/sucked, basically, where the Jammer goes, to die.

Awfully dramatic sounding isnt it?

Each Jam can last up to 2 minutes, with lead Jammer status, you have the power to call off the Jam early with a tap of both hands to the hips, a Jammer calls off a jam to stop the other team from scoring points, has been pushed out of the track or could simply be exhausted in the sad place and simply says 'enough.'

Sounds simple enough right?

Clear as mud.

While I could write a book on the technical aspects of the game (well I kinda am right now, I guess), the rules, positions, strategies and all that, the online google sites do it heaps better than I could.

Google WFTDA rule book/guide for endless rule confusion!

This book is more just a healthy fan based obsession with limitless adoration for my sport.... Just sayin....

I will totally add some links at the end of the book (great for if you are interested in the rules, reffing or Non - Skating-Oficialling).

And of course there are endless video footage of this awesome sport if you want to get a proper visual of some Derby action, You Tube is your friend.

Or even better get the real deal live action and seek out your local derby league, they can be found all over, we are everywhere.

What I wanted to emphasis here is that if you are interested in roller derby this book is for you.

I've also found that if you mention roller derby in conversation people will also become interested when you talk, its a curios type of sport and enquiring minds want to know.

Its different in that not everyone can do it and is not a typical taught in school sport (although that would be cool, and I totally would have chosen that as a kid, well the full contact part would possibly be frowned upon by parents, but hey, I can dream).

There is this curiosity and stigma attached to the sport, its not a gentle sport and others will ask questions if you do play, expect that, its a great opportunity to positively change peoples perceptions of the sport, also....
 YAY! Someone new to 'talk derby' to.

Roller Derby is a Conversation starter

Derby always gives you something to talk about, in particular, the roughness of the sport seems to be the theme – "oh I could never do that, I'd be too scared to be injured".

I would argue with anyone wanting to learn Derby, using fear as a blocker, to come skate with me, and if you are not having fun straight up, I will never mention derby to you again.

First off, in order to do the Derby you have to know how to skate and roller skating, equals = FUN.

We, the Derby peeps (or derby folk), would never consider making you join this sport unless you or a coach has given us the OK to do so; and you have passed basic minimum skating skills.

So lets debunk that myth straight up.

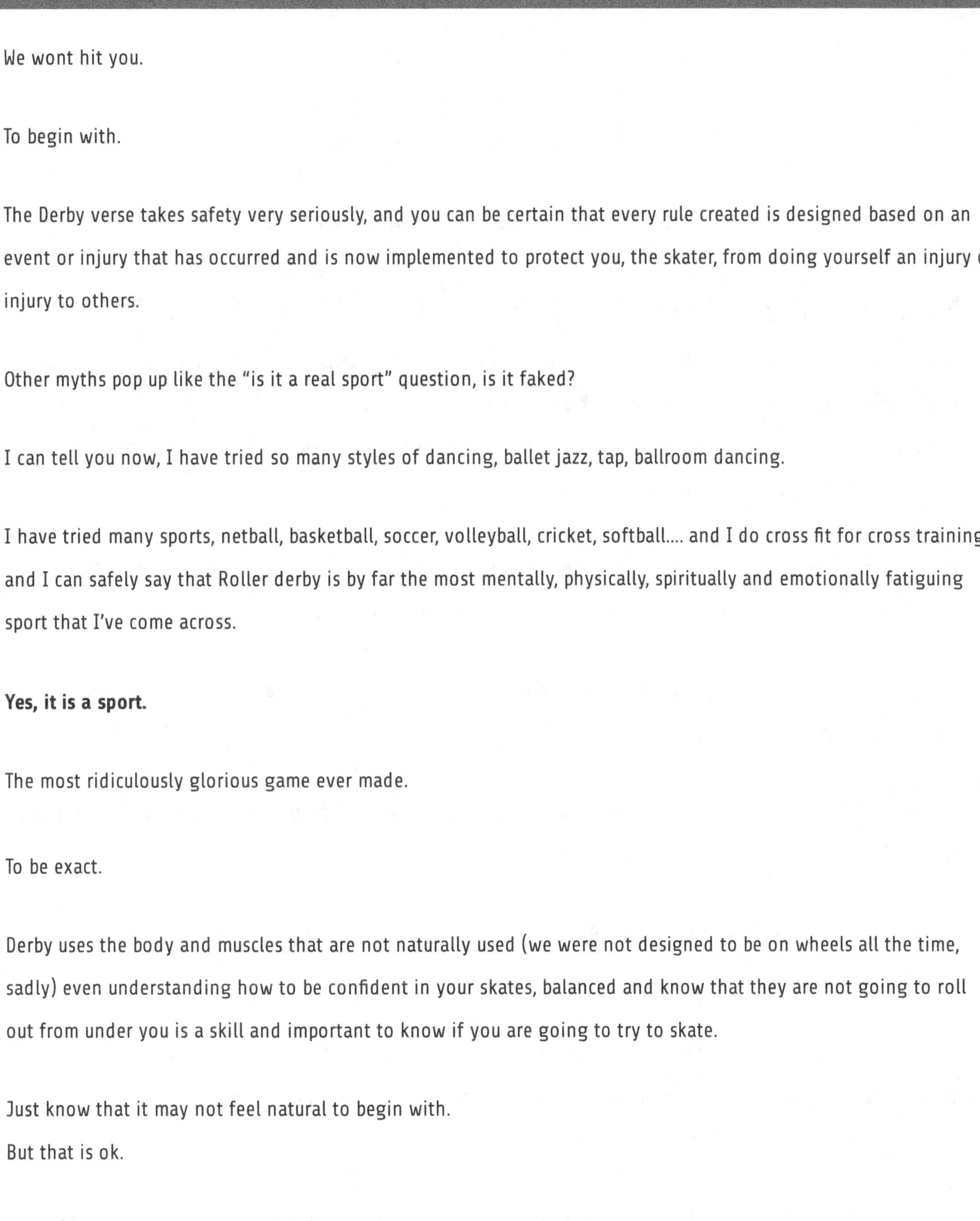

We wont hit you.

To begin with.

The Derby verse takes safety very seriously, and you can be certain that every rule created is designed based on an event or injury that has occurred and is now implemented to protect you, the skater, from doing yourself an injury or injury to others.

Other myths pop up like the "is it a real sport" question, is it faked?

I can tell you now, I have tried so many styles of dancing, ballet jazz, tap, ballroom dancing.

I have tried many sports, netball, basketball, soccer, volleyball, cricket, softball…. and I do cross fit for cross training; and I can safely say that Roller derby is by far the most mentally, physically, spiritually and emotionally fatiguing sport that I've come across.

Yes, it is a sport.

The most ridiculously glorious game ever made.

To be exact.

Derby uses the body and muscles that are not naturally used (we were not designed to be on wheels all the time, sadly) even understanding how to be confident in your skates, balanced and know that they are not going to roll out from under you is a skill and important to know if you are going to try to skate.

Just know that it may not feel natural to begin with.
But that is ok.

Roller Derby is not a sport for the faint of heart, and let me assure you friend, if you are in the presence of a derby person, you are soon going to understand what it means to be in the presence of greatness.

(I know that is an arrogant statement, but give me the chance to explain why I believe it with all of my 5'1" heart).

For a new roller derby person, you, friend, are about to become the hero of your own story.

Because every derby player has an origin story

 someone just recently asked me (another random curious admirer of the sport) how I got into Derby in the first place, what made me choose this as my sport and I smiled at the question.

Because I remember the first time I went to a skate fit class, I was just newly separated from my ex (after having been in a relationship for well over a decade).

I was now a single mum of 3 kids working full time and I was a little lost at how to fill this massive gap that was previously my partner (but that is entirely different book in and of itself:)).

I was a little depressed, over weight and I definitely felt the urge to reinvent myself a bit, figure out how I was going to navigate this new world I had found myself in So ....

I knew I wanted to do something new, something that would help me be healthier/fitter, but also something that didn't feel like going to a gym or doing actual exercise, I wanted to have fun.

I looked at things like kayaking, bike riding, nature hiking, but I would try them once and just kinda say Meh if I had to do it again, I had zero motivation.

I remember watching the movie 'whip it' (Awesome derby film) on a rerun, thinking now skating would be cool, I loved skating as a kid, at the local rink and derby looked bad ass (see chapter on Badassery) but seriously where was I going to learn to skate or play Derby?

I knew of a local ice skating rink but let the thought slide thinking that I would need to move to a city in order to actually learn to roller skate again.

Funnily enough, it was my ex partner who brought it to the forefront of my mind a few months later when he was dropping off the kids he says to me,

"Nikki I've found the perfect thing for you",

(alright I'll play along) "oh yeah?"

"Coffs Harbour has Roller Derby"….

"No way! I would know if Coffs has derby, I've lived here forever, (granted I moved away to uni for a few years, but still)
How have I not heard about this?"

"Well they have a Facebook page, if you wanted to have a look."

Ok google, work your magic; and universe, I get the message loud and clear, why hello Coffs Coast Derby you are having a sign up intake night in a week or so from now?

Coincidence?

I think not.

I rocked up to the sign up night a very nervous but also really excited human ready to roll.

After signing a disclaimer around injuries and asking if I would like to be resuscitated if knocked unconscious… (say what!?) I was geared up with helmet, knee pads, elbow pads (which I totally put on upside down), wrist guards and a pair of skates (note to self do not put wrist guards on before skates, problematic and unnecessarily annoying).

I was ready to go and it was absolutely………… terrifying.

The first week comes and the first lesson is about balance and how to fall and stop safely, the coach demonstrated what looked to me like you simply throw yourself to the floor, and then get up again............. my initial reaction?

Ya'll are crazy;

HELL NO!!!!!!

I tell my origin story to really emphasis the newness of a thing, which can be sometimes absolutely overwhelmingly dauntingly terrifying, and that that is an absolutely normal reaction to the situation.

(But back to the story)

In my head I was already playing the self doubt movie reel montage.

Why are you doing this?

Why would you think you can roller skate let alone play roller derby someday?

You are a grown adult for goodness sake!

Are you just having a mid-life crisis?

A full body contact sport, when you cant even stand straight up, or fall right?

Just FALL already!

I was watching others around me fall to their knees but truthfully my inner voice had taken control, my brain just kept saying nope, this is wrong.

Why would I deliberately throw myself on a hard wood floor?

Was this some weird Game of Thrones refusal to "bend the knee"?

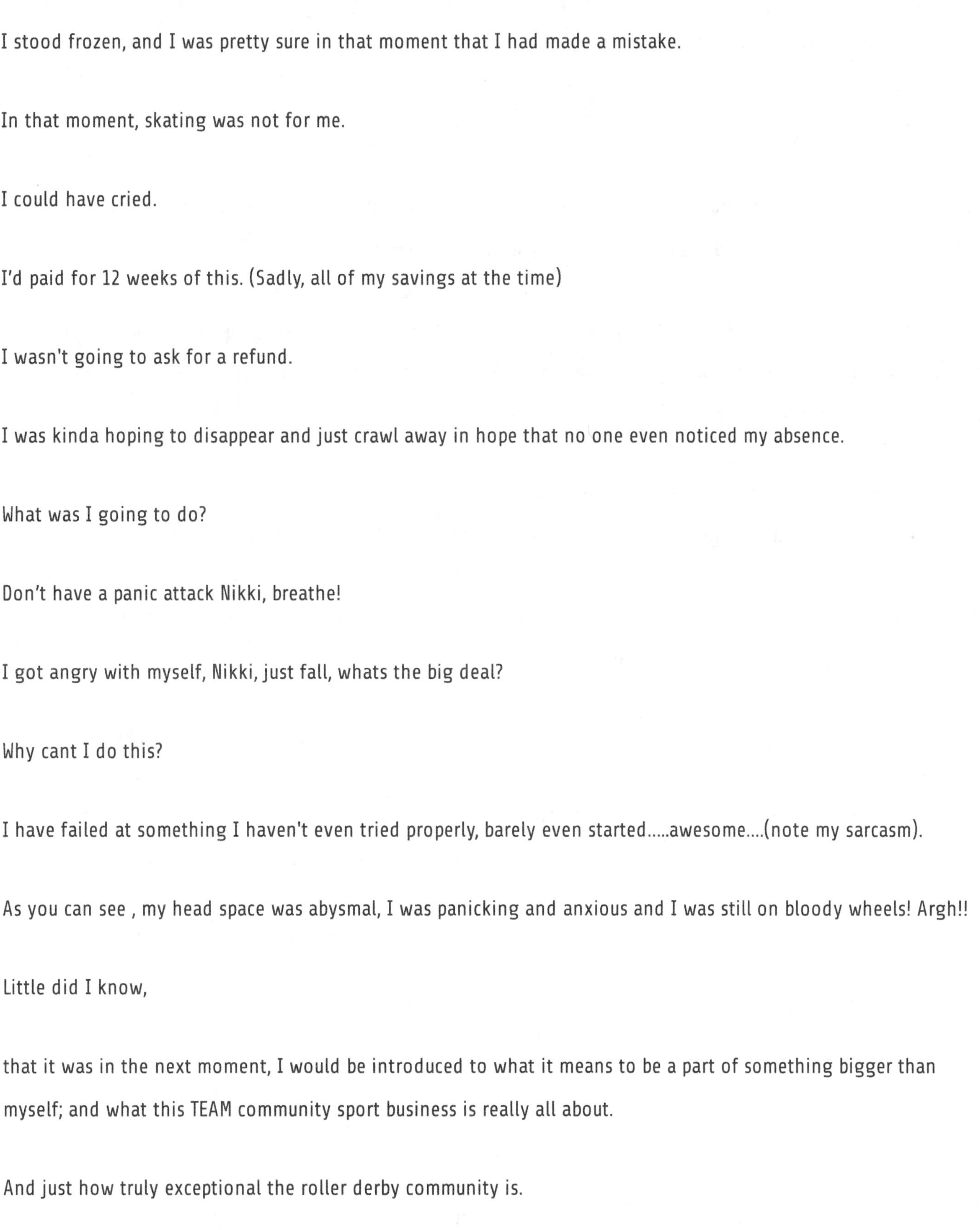

I stood frozen, and I was pretty sure in that moment that I had made a mistake.

In that moment, skating was not for me.

I could have cried.

I'd paid for 12 weeks of this. (Sadly, all of my savings at the time)

I wasn't going to ask for a refund.

I was kinda hoping to disappear and just crawl away in hope that no one even noticed my absence.

What was I going to do?

Don't have a panic attack Nikki, breathe!

I got angry with myself, Nikki, just fall, whats the big deal?

Why cant I do this?

I have failed at something I haven't even tried properly, barely even started.....awesome....(note my sarcasm).

As you can see , my head space was abysmal, I was panicking and anxious and I was still on bloody wheels! Argh!!

Little did I know,

that it was in the next moment, I would be introduced to what it means to be a part of something bigger than myself; and what this TEAM community sport business is really all about.

And just how truly exceptional the roller derby community is.

One of the coaches/skaters, came up to me, I'm pretty sure she didn't know my name and I couldn't remember hers, but she had a smile on her face and she said something to me along the lines of "how are you going, would you like some help?"

She said, "I know its not a natural feeling to deliberately fall and it might feel a bit awkward, but hey, we are grown adults on roller skates, we already look ridiculous, so you might as well give it a go."

She doesn't know (well she does now) that this comment let me release the tension and anxiety I was feeling; and laugh at how true her statement was, it got me out of my head and to breath she then proceeded to say "look how about we try this together?"

So the both of us went down on one knee slowly, then the other, followed by an elbow, then the other elbow and I was there on the floor, I had done it, I had let myself fall, it was easier than I thought and it felt kinda amazing.

Which was a feeling quickly dashed when then came the harder part, where the she than says "Ok, back up and try again" .... and again, and again and again.

I came to understand that in this sport its perfectly normal and fine to fall, all you have to do, is get back up.

This would not be the only time where my anxiety would cause problems, this happened for nearly every new skill that I had to learn for basic minimum skills (the skills that would be needed in order to play a game of roller derby)

For every new skating skill I would have the same frustrating process, I watched the others in awe, they made it look so easy, so natural.

I would say yeah nah,

that's impossible,

knee slides, thats totally wicked but I'm a mid thirties women for goodness sake!

Crossovers, put one foot in front of the other, nope slide it, nope lift the foot, one foot glide, i Cant one foot glide this shit is imppossible!

skating backwards (say what?)

transitions, (facing one way than another, this skill took 5 people to teach me)

Jumping!!!!! (FUCK NO!! These wheels aren't leaving the ground, are you crazy?) I still cant one foot glide!!!

Every step of the way, I tell you

I was terrified, but here's the kicker, my fear was nothing, when I had that (as the coach would say) 'ah ha' moment after doing the thing repeatedly until it felt normal. Until it clicked and my body learnt how to move on skates.

Until it felt natural.

And the best part.

There was always a coach, or a seasoned skater there, to pick me up or break through the mental and physical barriers of my fragile psyche to give encouragement or reassurance.

A community of people who sometimes, literally, lifted you up, with a few positive phrases, "you've got this', "I believe in you", "you're doing amazing" such simple statements and of course, I didn't believe them in the slightest to begin with, but eventually that positivism starts to rub off (well that could just be sweat actually), it seeps in and you start to think maybe,

just maybe,

I can.

The people from this community are most likely also facing their own 'obstacles' but because we all were here to do this thing that we love, any success, was the success of the group that was building.

Not only did I learn to fall, that happened quite naturally on its own, often, without any mental blocks from me.

But I learnt to get back up fast (gotta MuFasta) and keep going.

It would take a year for me to play my first game of Derby. That's my beginnings.....

What will your origin story be?

Falling forward – no sorries in derby

In derby we say, if your going to fall, fall forward, this results in less injuries, control the fall DON'T PLONK for this allows you to jump back up fast and also reduces the impact or distance with which you have to fall.

Keep your knees soft and GET LOWER, people (myself included) never think much of the get lower concept, im already hobbit size, how is getting lower going to help?

Well ….. the answer is simple, getting lower is a squat, squats are one of the most effective strength exercises around.

A squat will get you through your day, reduce the risk of injury and helps with mobility as you get older.

It strengthens core muscles and reduced impact on knees and ankles increasing bone density and thus reducing being injured if you do fall.

A squat will give you the chance to load your legs to create explosive movement to propel yourself further, faster and with more dynamic power.

Cool, GET LOWER

Falling forward – no sorries in derby

Momentum plays a part too, that you are already facing that direction (squatting), so fall with it, until it becomes natural to fall that way.

In roller derby we are often encouraged to try things the 'wrong' way just to see how it feels, we try every persons way of doing one manoeuvre just to see if it will work for one or all, too.

Or if that movement is unique to the skater.

In derby it is always about the foundations, in order to do the fancy footwork or amazing manoeuvres you need the solid stance first, the balance, the drive, to enhance skills and development.

But in order to do these amazing things with your body, it has to develop the movement and muscle memory that is required and if you don't repeat the movements you will lose the skill.

My coach often said that if you are falling you are pushing yourself (if you're not falling you're not trying hard enough!!!) improving yourself, and the more you do the more natural it feels to progress.

And there is always a next level to progress to, the learning is never over in Roller Derby.

Another funny concept in Roller Derby is that we say there are "no SORRIES in Derby," much like in the movie a league of their own "there's no crying in baseball."

If you see someone fall or get hit or you hit someone and fall over, or a combination of all of the above, the common reaction in normal circumstances would be to say sorry or ask if the person is ok.

While this is actually a really decent and kind thing to do in everyday circumstances, in derby it can cost you points or the game, or further injury if you are causing traffic jams on the track, the idea is to keep going, to let the refs call it or the skaters with the first aid/paramedics to decide whether the person is ok or not, do not get in the way.

I Know this sounds mean or unsportsmanlike, its contradictory to good sportsmanship....

but when you have new skaters on a track simply trying to remain upright on their wheels or don't know yet how to stop or fall correctly, stopping to check on a downed skater is a further disaster waiting to happen.

Also THIS IS ROLLER DERBY – you are supposed to make contact, make or take a hit from your friends and don't take it personally or feel targeted.

My general response is to feel impressed and also frustrated at the same time, for one that I let it happen at all (getting downed that is) and also in awe at the flying sensation of being landed with a solid hit, I give admiration where it is due – hot tip – when 'without a Trace' is on track you don't take the out or in, you go down the middle and pray someone on your offense can hold her long enough to go round. (see chapter on learning about your teammates)

Habits make practise perfect

I once read that we are what our daily habits consist of, no matter what we think or dream, at the end of the day it is in what we are doing on a consistent basis that really gives us insight and indicators into what it is we are about, where we are headed and what we can expect if we don't review our habits regularly.

When I realised this, I was terrified that I would be unable to learn new habits, but then again learning the new has never been the issue.

It is in the unlearning of old habits, ones we reach for, for security, or comfort when life gets tough, it is human nature.

In our chemistry to want to avoid pain and if our habits allow that, then yes it will be all too easy to fall back into them and it will feel natural even if somewhat disheartening.

Old habits need to be replaced with stronger habits, this is the only way to release the old to make way for the new.

Consistency becomes a friend in the creation of new habits, it needs to be small increments on a regular basis (daily if possible) one small example when looking at a sport like roller derby, for me the pleasure of skating takes precedent of any pain associated with becoming a skilled derby player.

I began with only 1 day a week for 12 weeks, followed by 2 days a week for 12 weeks.

I then joined a crossfit box and went to crossfit 1 day a week on top of the derby/skating.

Which soon led to 2, followed by 3-4.

I now aim to do 3 sessions a week crossfit and 2 a week derby/skating/training. Im not always successful in this, but the habit feels more natural now and I miss it when I don't get to the box or training for whatever reason.

Crossfit has now led to me looking at my diet and nutrition; and eating healthier (most days).

My point is that the happiness I gained from skating, soon outweighed all the negative bad habits I had formed, not exercising, poor diet, bad sleep.

And while I still work on all the areas to bring balance, being physically active helps that immensely.

I had found an intrinsic motivator in skating that was shaping all the areas in my life to something more positive and healthy.

I was becoming my own bloody hero of my story.

The main character so to speak.

That is the power of the Derby.

I couldn't believe how much motivation would come with wanting this, but I should also warn you that yes, there was struggle too, frustration at not being able to do the things, still after 3 months, 6 months, a year, 2 years, COVID, after injury.

Not having the best balance or coordination on skates.

Other things popped up for me too, the uncomfortable feeling of people being in my space physically.

Generally the only people I really touched in an affectionate way at the time were hugs to my kids and immediate family, watching these skater folks hip check, grab hips, pull on clothing, whip around, jump, push and pull each other, while it looked fun, wasn't necessarily something I was used to.

Or overly comfortable with.

I will talk about the derby smell later, (it gets its own chapter).

Derby is a full body contact sport, it gets pretty up close and personal on the track and having to rely on others to help, learning to push harder, dig in, block, be more aggressive (my pacifist self at war with the thrill of wanting to hit things) moving my body in ways it just hadn't moved before and I used to do ballet for goodness sake my body has done some crazy shit in its time.

It took some getting used to, though to really get up in other peoples spaces, its not a natural thing for me to deliberately put myself in front of a freight train coming at me and be encouraged to hit back with my body when someone gets up in my space.

Nobody ever really talks about it, the tactile nature of the contact, but also the brutality of it.

Yes, it hurts, I'm not gonna lie, it gets rough as, and do not be surprised or startled if you find yourself crying or frustrated or exhausted, or so sore you cant move.....emotional from a hit or emotional from a jam or a drill, sometimes this sport brings up or brings out emotions you didn't realise would impact you.

Give yourself the space to process this, and let the team be there for you, a lot of the people in roller derby are looking to gain strength in their lives, because they have felt or experienced or been overly exposed to vulnerability or trauma.

Roller Derby is a great sport for building resilience against overwhelming feelings.

crazily enough, this is ALL very 'normal'(whatever that means).

Built in community

I also never realised that joining this sport, I was not only getting a way to improve my fitness, learn a new sport/skill, I was joining an entire community of amazing people who were just as weird, awkward, quirky and completely into this thing as I was and that we all wanted to do together.

It was amazing to me that there were so many uniquely different types coming along, also it was the first time I had experienced an almost all female focused full bodied contact sport.

Generally speaking, it is not every day that you see a group of primarily female oriented (including LGBTQIA+ in that equation) willingly smashing into each other aggressively as a team.

There are several individual sports, MMA, UFC, boxing and women's sports leagues, that absolutely give space for women to be aggressive, but its not the norm; and the bonds that develop through this type of contact is interesting. (someone should totally write a psychological thesis on it, its fascinating….maybe one day).

One minute you are being hit and the next you are being given a hand up or a "you all good?" give me a thumbs up. The community is extraordinary.

The community also invests in other communities.

As a volunteer based sport, every person in the community is there because they want to be, there is no monetary gains to be had, generally all funds we make are put back into the league for insurance or space hire and if we do raise funds its either for a charity cause or to fund a travelling game.

We pay to play.

A derby league is run by a committee of volunteers that keep it all turning, if you are a part of the sport remember to stop and thank committee members, coaches, refs, Non skating officials, because these wonderful people are the reason we all get to play or watch this awesome sport.

They make this magic happen and without them, we don't have a sport.

Roller Derby, once a professional sport, we now mostly pay to play, but one day it will be professional again.

Committees spend a lot of time making sure everyone is safe and organised and seriously, these committees should run for politics and rule the countries, because they just get shit done.

Every time.

And I would happily trust that they would have the world sorted in a week, two tops.

Local and international league communities alike are extremely welcoming, I have made friends in the derby community with people from New Zealand, America, I even got to be coached at Derbyfest by Krissy Krash from the movie "whip it" itself, such a tops community, very far reaching and yet still close knit and small at the same time.

The camaraderie is astounding and sometimes overwhelmingly heartfelt, I do hope the team and coaches and members of the league I am in know that they have pulled me from depression and anxiety's edge many a times over the years, with a simple check in or a funny meme or chat or just asking "how was your week" with no expectation that the response will be good but rather a "oh it was shit? Good, lets go skate and hit each other about it"

Find the friendly side....

Friendship circles are a very natural part of human nature and roller derby is no exception.

If you love to skate or love the sport of roller derby and want to be a part of the derby verse all that is requested of you is to love an aspect of it and shazam, friends made for life.

You realise that when you are skating at speeds of feeling like flying about to collide with others that can be a 'freight train' of a feeling you want to look for your friendlies, the ones who will either get out of your way or help push you through.

The difference between friendships and teammates (see chapter on teammates) is something to be mentioned here, don't lose focus on the distinction.

If people are skating with you they want you on the team, honestly, if you are on a derby team, regardless of age or experience, if you are here to skate, willing to give it your best, you will be accepted.

Yes, you will grow to know and trust your team in Derby, you will be drawn to the like minded people who may or may not want to socialise with you outside of skating.

While it is imperative for the committee and team to be all inclusive for all skating events and social gatherings, if you are making friendships outside of that, or you are noticing that others are forming friendships outside of that, don't take it to heart or too personally.

This can lead to nothing but potential unnecessary heartbreak otherwise known as Derby Drama.

Or Derby politics.

Where there is a community of humans there will always be politics, differing personalities and belief systems. The best way to become a part of the community is to know your own strengths in the derby world as a skater.

What do you bring to the table?

What are you contributing?

My own example is that I try to learn every new skaters name fast, talk to everyone at each session if I can and find out what brings people to skating (everyone has an origin story)

As the newbie, expect to admire the camaraderie of the team, but don't worry too much just yet about that, learn to do the skating things first, that's what we're all here for after all, to skate, let that be your guide for building friendships.

Because believe me when I say the coaches and team will spot a willing skater a mile away and then the team will come to you, seduce you, entice you to join them...."ONE OF US"......
Ahem.... that took an interesting turn, but really though, friendships form when a team member realises you want in and they will bring you into the fold flawlessly and you get to be a part of this amazing thing you didn't even realise you wanted initially; then next minute you are holding on for dear life in the most adrenaline pumping thrill ride ever and you have a whole group standing beside or around you just as pumped to do this awesome thing again and again and again.

If like me, you are a bit socially awkward, you are among like-minded people and generally it will take time to get to know each other.

ROLLERDERBY-The most ridiculously glorious game ever made

What the team skaters will notice immediately, is if you are keen on skates, that you are turning up, that you are having a go, and that will bring acceptance far faster than any social interactions.

You want Talk about skating, talk about what you want from skating, I will guarantee there is always someone wanting to talk skating, skates equipment, gear, strategies, breaking down movements, favourite skate skills, favourite derby players, because from my own experience we are all big nerds (#fangirl) when it comes to this sport, it draws you in once you realise just how bad ass it is and there is merchandise and funny puns and argh im getting ahead of myself.

My point is you will find friendships among the community, just don't lose sight of why you're in the community, whether to skate, ref, NSO, volunteer, or just be a huge fan, know your reasons for loving the derby.

I say this because cultures can become quickly changed if people are feeling excluded, gossiped about, hurt egos can get in the way of the skating and it can take away from having a strong team.

Building a positive cultural environment is something I will get into more later.

A new found love of Fitness.....say what?

What is that smell?

Well crap, its me, the derby STANK, literally.

I had never sweated so much in my life. And why do i now own so much active wear? this is madness i tell you, MADNESS!!!! :)

I happen to have an overly sensitive sense of smell and my first time at team training had me sweating out my eyeballs, it hit me as kinda gross to begin with, especially that my sweat was mingling with others sweat (gag) it took some getting used to much like the contact.

While I thought the smell and sweat were bad, the gear smell is a whole other leave of nauseating sometimes it literally hits me with the pungent smell of vomit inducing derby stank – but also, part and parcel of the sport. What i wasn't prepared for was the sheer exhaustion and toll taken on my body, it was something completely different, unusual, was it normal to hurt this much and be this sore?

I remember the day after my first skating session, I couldn't walk comfortably up and down stairs or get on and off the toilet without tensing at the squat pain.

I had no idea that roller skating would leave me so physically exhausted, I also thought foolishly that doing skating twice a week was going to make me fit. That i wouldn't need to do other things to improve my skating abilities.

Attending a roller derby festival about 6 months in, quickly revealed that I was no where near past a beginner level – and that I was most definitely, not fit.

It was at the 6 months mark and I thought I should be better already, but looking at people who had been skating for over 5, 6,10 years, you start to realise that you have a long way to go, to really get where your hoping for, but I will tell that story a little more in depth later on.

Derby is not a simple sport, while it looks like nothing more than a clustered mess of bodies barging into each other, there is a method and strategy in the madness, and it is a sport that requires a decent clear mind to stay focused.

Fitness did not come easily to mc, however, what did come, was the motivation I mentioned before, I didn't sigh or not feel like going to skating.

It was the opposite actually, I found myself waiting to skate, and all the time in between was taking too long.
For me it was an hour or 2 without children to do a thing I loved, I had found a happy place and the bonus was that it was motivating an inner determination to become fitter and healthier so I could do this thing that I loved, better. I didn't just want to do some skating and think that that was enough.

No, what I was seeing others do, I wanted that, I also for the first time ever, wanted to be a better me.

I wanted this for myself, for no one else, to determine what that looked like for me, to find out if I had what it takes to get better, to be better, to listen to what the coaches were saying and really put into practise the things that would help me become a great skater.

But not only this, I wanted to be a roller derby player, a roller derby athlete.

First things first – The skating part

On top of learning a new sport, the greatest skill by far would have to be how much fun can be had on a pair of roller skates on a derby track and off track, I've learnt new skills in park skating and trail skating, ice skating and just the various activities I can now do with confidence and determination on a pair of skates.

The skills I have gained has really opened the doors to confidence in so many other areas of my life as well and especially in areas I had never even considered.

For instance since learning to skate I not only play derby but also I have entered cross fit competitions, been more assertive at work which has led to a permanent management position.

I don't say this to impress anyone, but more to explain what confidence building in skating has done for me in all the varying aspects of my life.

The positive and successful impact happened because of this one life decision to learn to skate, which has positively ripple effected all areas of my life.

Its also a foundational place to go when I need to clear my head, feeling life's stress or overwhelm.
Skating makes everything feel better.
It clears the mental load like nothing else has for me before.
It always starts with the slow rolling, feeling the ground beneath my feet just glide away and all the worries in the world disappear and I fly.

Learning to skate, was really difficult, but what it meant was that I can learn other things too.

But skating first, if you want to play roller derby the first thing you have to learn is how to stand in your skates followed very quickly by learning to stop and fall safely.

All other skills will come after this.

You get a Coach

I had never had a coach before, I had had plenty of teachers and learnt many things from them, but the difference between what a teacher does and what a coach does is very distinct.

Coaches really opened my eyes to how much potential lives within an individual, I learnt how much more I had to give this world.

I admit I had (and still do have) self limiting beliefs and in the beginning, rather low self esteem.

What having a coach did, was give me a new dialogue to have as an inner voice that changed and reshaped the negative self talk.

Having someone in my corner, believing in me, when I mostly didn't believe in myself.

I have had up to 7 skating/derby coaches now (not including teammate advise and cross trainers).

I have found that each one has brought something out of me I didn't realise I was lacking or not utilising to my strengths or holding back from.

It is the strangest feeling having a person who truly believes that you are capable of reaching new levels of skills/performance/greatness whatever the goal is really.

I have had coaches be the motivating voice in my head, remind me to not take myself so seriously, step it up, remind me that I can and do, often.

Coaches have schooled me on my language, I did a thing, not attempted to do a thing.

Coaches have reminded me that I am getting stronger, faster, some have pulled me from a depression spiral (on multiple occasions) told me to get lower, be more precise, keep going, you've got this, I believe in you, get up, get up, get up, up, up, up keep going, keep going, get up.......well you get the idea.

Coaches are motivating and determined to get you where you need to be, sometimes you may not even know where or what that looks like, but they know, because they have either done it for themselves and are showing you the way, or they have seen it and brought it out of others before and know its just a matter of time before the pattern emerges again.

Coaches also know where you struggle, they know when your having an off day, a good day, they just know and when they don't, they interrogate you (in a nice way of course) they check in, they ask about other areas of your life because they are determining your focus, your motivation, and they do all this sometimes, I think, without even realising how awesome they are.

If you are fortunate enough to have a good coach, ever, say thank you, but be specific, let them know what is working and let them know how awesome they are. Often.

I recently attended a 'beginner' level scrim and the most amazing thing began to happen on the track, it didn't actually matter which player was on track I found myself cheering for the other team when I realised just how exhausted they were.

I heard myself yelling, "get back up, you've got this, yes you can" and I wanted to kinda cry at how full circle that moment was.....

of course this was followed by some epic falls (by me) but remember my fall story, that in the beginning, I couldn't, my fall reel now is notorious, I fall over myself, over others, over the air and it is always ridiculous, but what continues to be noticed by others is not the hilarity of the fall (still a pretty good laugh though) but the fact that I roll, slide, dive, stumble tumble and it doesn't matter, I'm back up quick smart.

Except when I break my ankle, of course.... But more on that story later.

Back to the coach, belief in another, is the power of the coach, if you have never had a coach before I suggest you get one, for whatever part of your life you are wanting to delve into or make a change with or improve on, a coach will get you there.

Having someone on your side, in your corner, whose already done the work, knows what you are feeling and is right there with you, holding you to account, telling you that you will get through it, you cant help but push yourself, and soon you find yourself pushing your limits and mind and body further than you ever have before and you know its because you have this coach voice in your head.

They have the faith and belief in you because they know you can and they have the confidence in you to back it up.

Cant say it enough, coaches are bloody awesome!!!

I say this this with a humbleness, in that I recently coached a skatefit class while the other coaches were away; and I felt very much like a substitute teacher (a fun one hopefully) but the confidence and reassurance that good coaches exude, I'm in awe of that.

New Self esteem

"Ok so imma gonna get real with ya'll for a sec"

My self esteem coming into skating was pretty shit, as I already mentioned, I had many self limiting beliefs, not to mention I was pretty reserved in letting people into my life, I was just here to skate, that's all.

I find that a lot of people come to Roller Derby because they are going through something that requires them to make great change in their life (I'm no exception, cough** newly angry single parent looking to fill a void cough**)

Roller Derby finds the skater when it is needed and gives a person the perfect outlet to really find an inner strength; confidence and power to continue on with what they are looking for in life.

Roller derby brings with it health, skills, resilience building; and it does this by demanding you work on yourself to improve, it demands you learn to be hit and hit back, to fall down again and again until the air is crushing your lungs and the sweat is pouring into or out of your eyeballs and you have given it your absolute all.

And then your expected to get back up and keep going regardless of the exhaustion.

Derby demands athleticism, it demands trusting yourself and others, it demands some fearlessness and also perhaps a little craziness.

And because of all of this, your self esteem will improve, because you will feel stronger, you will feel healthier, you will feel more confident in your own body and self (I get a kind of thrill and villainess smirk when I notice this change in new skaters, a set determination, a change in the way they hold themselves) its like out of the movies when you know something amazing is about to happen and the anticipation is building and you get to watch it unfold...

It reminds me of a Simpsons episode where there is a mafia fight happening in the front yard and one of the people are just standing still and Marge says "lets get inside Homer" but Homer is like "But Marge, He's Gonna Do Something! And You Know It's Gonna Be Good" its that feeling, only in this instance you get to be both the cool mafia guy and Homer at the same time and it just.....it is super hard to explain the love of something that is both ridiculous and glorious in equal measure.

Following that feeling with higher self esteem comes greater confidence, for me its that I get to be taller on skates (I am a forever hobbit).

I cant quite place the wording, but there is something in the way Derby has grit and grunge but also swagger, when you skate you can roll with more confidence when you play roller derby and are hitting bodies on the regular, mundane everyday other tasks seem easier, almost laughably so.

With a team backing you and going through this with you as well, you have more courage, more strength, to find your own style of expression, speaking up against injustices, finding your voice and courage to use it, defending your team and others both on and off the track.

Suddenly you have the confidence to not hold back, not hesitate, voice your opinion, wear that raunchy outfit, tell someone to stuff it.

And not just on the track but in your day to day living.

I say all this in relative terms, I would never suggest derby gives you the power to give your boss the finger, but you start to observe the people around you and you start to see who is good for you, who is trying to gain something from you or who is genuine.

You find yourself having the courage to question others actions.

Roller Derby is also a challenge, there is elements so challenging that other obstacles soon become rather silly in comparison.
For example, I spent a training session just pushing against a wall that felt like it went on for hours. The next day at work writing a report within a deadline just seemed easier (a different skillset, yes) the mindset on what I considered difficult now has shifted and what is challenging to me now takes on new meaning and focus.

I would say, that it is a sport that promotes leadership, because it is an aggressive sport, and it is a type of aggression that it creates an emotional impact on others.

A type of aggression that takes risks.
Like in day to days, it gives you the courage to maybe go for that promotion, or ask for a pay rise.

This is its uniqueness, aggression can be found everywhere, but this type of aggression in sports is rare and often frowned upon (in particular from a woman's perspective), which makes it all the more important and necessary.

I have found that the sport has changed my confidence, by giving me both intrinsic and extrinsic motivators, its made me reach for goals I never even knew I wanted for myself, for instance I can dead lift more than 20kgs more than my own body weight right now.

Why do I need to do this? I have no idea, but I don't care, I'm still bloody impressed with myself for being able to do that.

Developing healthy self beliefs and esteem is no easy feat when you are overcoming limiting beliefs and I talk more later on that it took 2 communities for me to learn to change my mindset around what my true limits and potential was.

Building self esteem takes time, and learning to skate and play roller derby also takes time, take note of how the progressions of both develop in complement to each other.

Teamwork – learning about your skater peeps

I am contemplating writing a whole other book on team work and the magics that come with being a part of an awesome team of people, because I had no idea how having people in your life that genuinely not only want you to succeed, but help you get there as fast or slow a pace that you are wanting (or they believe you are ready for) because they are right there with you going through this experience with you, its extraordinary.

A group of people that believe in you and will reassure you that they believe in you, sometimes literally picking you up off the piled heap you have become on the ground, and if you cant get back up they will lay beside you in exhaustion too, or hold your hand through the pain.

It is sending funny gifs to let people know that "we've got you" its letting each other know that we are about to shit ourselves in fear of real life derby game play together – and we are fully supportive of each other in this endeavour.

On a track, you have 4 other people on your team in that moment, which, for that 2 minutes, are your life line, like you are theirs, so communication is key, they need to know where you are what you are doing, what the other team is doing.

Is the bench coach yelling at us?

Have the reffs called a penalty?

Where's the bloody pack?

Where's the jammer?

Did we just block our own jammer?

Oh for fuck's sake!

This game teaches you the importance of effective communication, because so many things are happening all at once.

Whether through being overly vocal, using code words or gesturing like a mad wild gyrating wildlings, open communication is a must in roller derby.

If you have a problem with a team mate you talk it out, talk it through.

Share ideas, celebrate progress and celebrate goals achieved.

Also grieve through the losses and frustrations together, create new determination to set new goals and as a team know the plan to get you all there together.

The team will usually have a goal in mind, building a team, preparing for a game, learning a new strategy.

Team bonding activities are a great way to break the ice with the group.

Derby is after all, a full body contact sport, getting up close and personal physically is a normal part of the sport, but even this can be daunting to people who have never really experienced this type of aggressive contact before.

It is a real fear, and I can say with all the dignity I can muster, that I have had several teammates just simply stomp their foot (skate) near me and I high pitch squeal like a teenage fan girl at a one direction concert as just a reflexive response (they know who they are and will hopefully one day teach me their Jedi mind tricks).

As well as all that, don't forget, you are all still on wheels as well, so even your balance and sense of gravity is in constant flux and motion; and you have to be really aware of how your body stands in skates and build the confidence in going from feeling like a Bambi on ice to a gliding gazelle.

Literally, you will often be leaning on your team, and while yes you want to be strong in your skates this game cannot be played alone.

I found it hard in the beginning to rely or lean on my team mates because I am a fiercely independent person, but I learnt very fast that I needed and wanted all the bodies I could muster around me to either stop the opposing team or helping me through walls of bodies.

I end up stuck in the sad place, a lot.

The team is who free me from there, and when they do im so relieved I often forget that instead of stopping to say thank you I hear them screaming "go, go, go…. Oh yeah, still skating have to get around the track haul ass, nope took too long stuck behind another bum really do gotta MuFasTa.

Being part of a team also means that you bring your strengths to the table, each member of the team will contribute to the end goal or actions needed.

Being part of a team means you understand where you need to be and what you need to do as a member of that team, trying new things is great in practise and training, but trying something new on game day is not going to help the team.

Being part of a derby team gives you a sense of belonging, you are making a commitment to build each other up as a group.

Team members are always happy to assist others with ideas and suggestions, if a team member is struggling with a skill, I found that talking to a few different teammates how they learnt/do the derby thing, I get a better grasp of how many different ways it can be done and I figure out how best that works for me.

Derby is interesting in that you can develop as an individual but the team will really hone in on where your strengths lie.

One of the awesome aspects of this sport is that everyone is different, all shapes and sizes that will have a unique style on skates. And there in lies where the playing field is evened, everyone is on wheels, and everyone has a centre of gravity in this game, no one is exempt from falling or getting tired, eventually.

Understanding the diversity and then adapting to the physics of that style of skating is a real skill.

I once attended a great Derby workshop called "the ME in TEAM" I thought this was great because it was about embracing your own unique style as a skater, by knowing your strengths and understanding how that will work into the team and game play.

Listening to your team both on and off the track is another great skill, asking them what works for them is golden.

A strong team also usually has a leader that they look to (the captain usually).

This individual can be a coach or captain or a teammate, essentially it can be anyone, but what they do is work at being the glue holding the team together, they are responsible for setting the energy of the training session, offers encouragement and motivation to everyone, they check in on teammates, and keeps all members of the team updated on happenings.

I know that sounds like a lot, but it actually occurs quite naturally, also it shifts between people sometimes but you will notice that if the leader is having a down/bad day the session could be a little flat.

Its on those days that another team mate should check in on the leader.

But lastly and most importantly, teammates know how to have fun!!

Building positive relationships with teammates makes for a relaxed and positive cultural environment, also it's a great team bonding experience to simply laugh with each other often about the silliest of things.

The culture

Because of the natural progression of learning skate skills the culture of a team will ebb and flow as skaters come and go.

Creating a positive cultural environment takes time, effort and energy.

Its getting to know individuals and then giving them the space to figure out where they fit within the team.

Toxic cultures can quickly occur in team sports if athletes are shown favouritism or if team mates present with an over abundance of arrogance or ego.

This is a double edged sword or balancing act as a team you want each player/skater to be confident and competitive with an opposing team while also working together cohesively and also improving and progressing skills together.

This can be challenging for the team that are performing at different levels or are at various stages of their skating abilities, a good point of reference is to remind the team that they are only as strong as their weakest skater.

Working to bring each other up faster, through positive reinforcement and reassurance until the team is on par with each other.

And continue to progress.

Looking at different methods of building team culture there are several ways to bring the positivism about:

Praise each other, if you see something awesome, say something awesome.

Build each other up, be confident in each other, trust is built over time and only through the repetition of deliberately focusing on looking for the positive will this feeling of camaraderie build.

Help each other up, in derby we fall down, a lot. But not just on skates, sometimes we could be having a bad day or a bad week, month, year, Covid.

The team becomes a place of comfort, a place of safety where "hitting" your friends is acceptable and welcomed.

The intensity that is needed for derby requires stamina, endurance and mad athletic skills, you cant do this shit alone, you need your team, so let them help.

Check in when they fall down, I try to give a thumbs up when im down, in training, it lets the team know I'm ok usually.

focus on strengths, work on the weak spots until they too, become strengths

Have both individual and team goals (and know each others goals and hold each other to account).
Creating team goals is the easy part, every one wants to build skills and team dynamics, the hard part is putting the goals into action and then holding yourself and your team accountable to get to that place.

Accountability to yourself is not always easy, self analysis and reflection can be hard.

It is easy to make excuses, "I'm too tired, old, late"... and so on.
It is also easy to blame others for inaction, "if my parents had never separated, if we weren't so poor all the time, if I had the money, time, energy.........and so on....
The excuses are easy, and when you have conversations with others the excuses will be accepted.
Except when you are a part of a team, your teammate wont let the excuse stand, they will challenge it.

Having a team gives you an accountability buddy/buddies who wont let the excuses sway them.

Holding yourself to a goal or an outcome can also be a fearing motivator and while it can be terrifying, telling another person to not let you forget this, to have someone who would be disappointed if you didn't keep going, is also a tough gig, but can be motivating.

An accountability buddy reminds you why you started in the first place, they encourage you, support you, reassure you, that you can.

Being someones accountability buddy can be just as hard, being responsible for another persons goal or dream, with them, can also be exhausting.

I don't recommend doing this unless you have the space for this role, mentally, physically, spiritually and emotionally. Let the team know where you are up to in your own development before taking on the goals of others.

Because your person may get angry at you holding them to account (remind them that they put you in this role too).

Being your own accountability buddy can also be really difficult, on the one hand you can be too lax or in its opposite, too rigid, having a person even know your goal and telling them your own expectations and having their backing helps.

If you choose to be your own accountability buddy write down the expectation, the goal, the time frame, and also the consequence of what will happen if you don't reach this goal.

Communicate!
Talking with each other, celebrate every win no matter how small with each other, your success is their success and vice versa.
The team is succeeding, celebrate.
Encourage team experiences and build tradition and community.
Give feedback on how you will go about doing the things better next season together!

But most importantly in roller derby you must remember the most important thing about being a teammate, you are all there to HAVE FUN and LAUGH often.

empowerment

GOOGLE says that empowerment is – "the process of becoming stronger and more confident, especially in controlling one's life and claiming one's rights"

Roller Derby does this in a myriad of ways.

Firstly by delivering a skills based program to get from never having skated before to feeling confident on skates, to developing the fitness, confidence and mindset of what it takes to play roller derby.

Derby delivers on breaking down stereotypes and provides a space to learn ongoing life skills.

One such skill is how to maintain health and self care through skating type exercise.

One of our coaches is also studying to be an Occupational Therapist.

And while she lets us know all the overly long names of the anatomy that she has had to memorise, she also teaches us to focus on how to incorporate this into every day living.

Giving us tools to continue to provide us with a longevity of health and mobility as we get older.

We don't bend over to pick something up, we squat, we dont walk while we vacuum, we lunge with purpose.

We bend at the knees "we get low, not hoe"

We have people of all ages also come along to get their skate on and having an understanding of the physical toll and impact skating can have can sometimes (no matter how old) come as a bit of a shock.

When you are first make contact with a person, it can be unnerving, if you have never hit or been hit by someone before.

What eventually happens is you realise that you don't just have to be hit, you can hit back, and this direct type of aggression is actually really honestly refreshing.

Exhausting, but also exhilarating.

Healthy aggression

It is often noted that women tend to engage in more indirect forms of aggression (rumour spreading, gossiping, exclusion of an individual, body shaming or clothes monitoring) which is why roller derby is a fantastic platform for the progression of more direct female athletic aggression.

This direct **consensual** form of aggression (full body contact) has not generally been overly socially acceptable, or expected to a traditional gender normative audience, where in most female aggressive sports, women are expected to maintain an expected positivism, derby promotes an authenticity of the individual athlete, the sports gives freedom to really step into a full range of emotional diversity including frustration and anger.

While Derby promotes a positive attitude to sportsmanship and safety it also gives the athletic nuances to also be the villain (get in that big hit) the audience will "oh and ah" with the team.

The great thing about this sport is that it advances the ever growing change towards gender fluidity and steps away from traditional gender types.

Where previously roles dictated the cliched 'men were violent' and 'women were docile' is now becoming more androgynous, with a focus on the athleticism rather than the gender, something roller derby has always been before its time in its way of thinking.

An aggressive female athlete is no longer exhibiting 'masculine' behaviours but rather exhibiting athleticism.

A word of caution to the new skaters....

It is completely normal for this type of aggression to feel strange in the beginning, it can be intimidating, overwhelming, emotional and even triggering.

I say this in the face of my own personal experience.

There is an initial shock factor the first time you take a hit, the first time you get knocked down, there is a moment where you check,

am I alive?

Am I injured?

Was I flying?

Are all my body parts in the right order?

And woah that was awesome!!

not always in the same order

these thoughts take all of 2 seconds before you are rolling your way back to your feet, and you hear the team yelling "back up, up, go" at you and you are still just trying to find your bearings.

I wont say to you there are not times you want to just yell and swear and roll off the track and not come back but the thrill and adrenaline have you back soon enough.

Also the team around now starts the encouraging talk "keep going, come on you've got this, keep at it, keep going" and suddenly you find yourself back on track either defending or offending something with renewed vigour.

Leadership

I touched on leadership when I spoke of confidence and even being a leader-type team mate but I feel it needs its own heading and mention because it takes a certain level of confidence to participate in this sport.

It takes initiative, focus and fast decision making on track, a derby player needs to be assertive in strategic vision.

They need to be loud and focused.

The derby player needs to have an observation awareness that is impeccable, for you can be blindsided, sideswiped have tunnel vision or just be plain stuck in the sad place.

This type of awareness develops as you progress as a skater and get enough game time to actually discover the ins and outs of what it takes to play and understand the flow of roller derby.

Leadership is required because timidity and meekness have no place on a derby track.
That is just a disaster waiting to happen or worse, you become a target.

I say this from personal experience as one of the most shy, awkward, agreeably passive, submissive types you will ever meet off track.

The other team will find your weaknesses and exploit them ruthlessly. .

I am not an assertive or overly confident person generally, but I have learnt that I can be if I need to be; and I can choose when to reveal that part of myself and to who; and my favourite place to do so is the derby track.

I have no issue with attempting and often do look completely ridiculous on skates, stuff it up, go to hit someone and just totally bounce off that person or fly past them missing the target completely (my coach compares me to an annoying chihuahua and I have the fang teeth mouth guard to match that vibe).

Leadership tends to form also when you have new skaters on the team, you become quite protective of your new skaters, wanting to keep them from feeling overwhelmed while also bringing up their skills with you to be effective on track.

Healthy body imaging

What I absolutely love about Derby is that all body types are welcome to play, you can be any shape or size and bring something amazing to the game.

Its about what the body can do, not what it looks like

Roller Derby is known for a lack of body shaming, players encourage the show of skin and just being confidently in your body – you are on roller skates, your body is already doing strange things, embrace the vision of yourself you want to encompass in all your unique glory. You are the only you in this world, own that, bring it to life, and be proud of your body – its doing wild shit on skates, you are amazing!!!!

It took me a while to not be intimidated by the fact that I am an incredibly short person, who sometimes finds themselves in front of rock solid walls of men and women of various shapes and sizes.

I wont sugar coat it, it can be intimidating.

What really helped me though was the realisation that should have hit me a whole lot sooner. And I sound like a broken record but....
Everyone playing is on roller skates, everyone has a centre of gravity; and as a short person mine is lower.

I have discovered that shoulders to the ribs or hips to the stomach power centres are just as effective at putting someone off balance then a tall or bigger person will have to get lower if I choose to duck under them.

And little people can (which I take full advantage of and often take immense enjoyment in) just be, really fucking annoying :)

Derby really is the best.

It is an all inclusive sport men and women and others can play together in this sport (while yes men may have to adapt their impact levels) we are all on an even playing field because (and I cant emphasis this point enough) we are all on wheels...even a big burly bloke has a centre of gravity when on skates.

Because the game is also played both offensively as well as defensively there is numerous strategies to deal with all the different types of skaters and types on the track.

Optimus Grime (see link in references for pure awesomeness) developed a study of skating types/styles by comparing types of skaters to the movie avatar: the last air bender (air bender, earth bender, etc) emphasising the movements of styles that can be taught and adapted to if you know what style you are working with (or against) of course I learnt about this at DerbyFest.

It was awesome.

I also met another great coach who was teaching how to counter all the elements, it was a riot and a lot of fun.

I mention some of these wonderful people because every derby player I come across has amazing qualities within them (see heading chapter AWESOME people)

Alter ego's

In derby, while promoting empowerment and leadership, derby also has a sub cultural history of being able to entertain the crowd.
Because again remember we are all on skates and hey if you have the skating skills why not show them or use them to your gaming advantage.

In this sense you can use your own name or create a whole new persona in Roller Derby.

Much like a stage name, you can become on the track, all the things you might not be in your day to day, you can get angry and aggressive, you can yell and scream and the crowd will go wild with you.

You can be the hero or the villain or the secret weapon, there are endless possibilities with how you want to create or recreate yourself on the track.

In the history and origins of Derby it was very much like the World Wrestling and every member of the team was a particular character, a personality type and the name was usually a pun on words or other characters; and this quirky aspect has remained and followed through to today and it is just a fun aspect to the game.

I loved this sub cultural aspect because it gives a person a freedom to recreate themselves on the track.

For myself personally, I am shy in groups and not overly outspoken, but Derby gives me a safe space to explore different sides to my own personality, it brings a grungy type of freedom that was in correlation with the punk era along with the pinup styles or 20's but more on subcultures in the next chapters.

I found various inner alter egos emerged as I progressed with skate skills. I also found interesting mental mindsets when playing.
One such mindset came from a conversation I had with a skater by the name of 'Glam Cracker' Glam said to me "you have to leave your soul off the track", so that skaters cant have it, or wont take it from you, because that's what the other team wants to do.

Break you, suck your soul, don't let them, just leave it off the track, and because yours is not available on track, you can now take theirs....

While I was a little taken aback by the ferocity and macabre nature of this conversation, it stuck with me, and as I stand on the jammer line sometimes I think of this and an evil smile starts to form on my face and weird things do start to happen.
When I think of playing with this mentality, when I play "soulless" it actually becomes quite manic, I begin to laugh hysterically when I get hit or knocked down, this emotional dysregulation is both off putting and amusing to others but also a highly effective distraction of strategy.

The coach and team is often highly entertained by my laughing antics, but I wonder if its a response to the over stimulus?

Someone should write a research/thesis on the varying mentalities of the derby player....

Maybe some day... (an offshoot project for another time).

These other mentalities can also bring out the athlete, as a team sport it brings out competitiveness and aggression along with attitude or villain like qualities, there is a cheekiness, an in your face I could punch you or kiss you, slap your butt or cartwheel on skates or all of the above.

There is something for everyone in this sport.

I find that a lot of the subcultures or diverse minorities explore the life of roller derby, many are fringe dwelling types, think the cliché steam punk, punk, pin up 50s, gothic like wildlings, think Harley Quinn, biker rock, anyone from the LGBTQIA+ community, think the shy quiet librarian who is also a dominatrix, the park skater, circus performer, artists, musicians doctors....i could continue for pages....but now combine all those elements and you have yourself a derby player.

Derby pulls from many pop cultural fandom and cliché niches, you want to be a fairy, awesome.

A scary fairy, even better.

You want to wreck havoc on the world "Rika Havok" has you covered, a sniper on the track, a wrecking ball, or the chookie MONSTER its all here on the track for you to witness.

A derby team has so many characters and personalities that all kind of blur and blend but at the same time are so uniquely individual it is a fascinating thing to observe.

There are hidden treasures amoung the derby folk.

I have not met a one that doesn't display this quirk, this unique extraordinary-ness.

It hurts my heart sometimes at how great these humans are.

Every single one of them.

Its Badass

With all the reboots, remixes and remakes happening in the world right now, I love that during a global pandemic roller skating has had a resurgence!!

And with that, a renewed interest in roller derby.

Derby is not a gentle sport, or skill to develop; and as much as one can be eased into certain movements, it takes grit, and it is rough to your body, there is no delicate way to hip check someone on a pair of skates, there is no polite way to smash through a wall.

It is confronting and intimidating and a skater needs to bring an attitude (mines a misdirection of im a small hobbit person, don't pick on me..... but if you do decide to hit me... know that I wont be the only one going down, I'm taking you with me.... Just sayin...I eat second breakfast.

While yes derby does have a sense of etiquette of sorts (don't be a d!*k) and rules around target areas for safety, there is still a lot of body parts that are free game and you are going to get hit, you are going to fall over, often.

To think you can avoid that is to ask yourself am I here to play derby or in the highly inappropriate words of Johnny from the new awesome reboot of karate kids – Cobra Kai "are you a pussy?"

And while this may be a little crass or blunt, the reality is this is not a sport for the soft of heart, but it has heart, it takes guts and fearlessness and a just a pinch of crazy (or genius) to be willing to do the Derby things.

At the end of all the talk of roller derby I have to remember the best part.

The LAUGHTER and fun!!!!

I have never played a sport before where I found myself laughing so often, most especially at myself, but also just at the antics that a team gets up to when learning a new skating skill or strategy and the first few dozen times that the timing just doesn't match and then that one time that does.

Also there is always someone who wants to go skating, some one to talk to joke with and just plain be silly with.

When I talk to beginner skaters my ending question at the end of a class is "did you have fun?" or "what did you find the funnest?"

I do this because everyone's perspective is different, everyone takes something different from this sport, some hold onto the social aspects, some love the culture and subcultures, some like jumping or backwards or knee slides, everyone has their aha moments that just brings the smiles and you watch as a fire starts, a knowing that we just got (in an uncult like manner) another skater for this awesome sport.

GAME DAY!!!!

ok.....so....

you wake up excited, you have already put together your outfit, hmm, costume, ah uniform????

Well it could be any and all of the above.

You could be the sporty athlete who wears sensible bike pants and a fitted team shirt.

But you could also wear glitter or a tutu or pull out the fishnets and go goth or emo or punk or viking warrior or

well.....

whatever takes your fancy really, also does your game day have a theme?

Because yes that could determine your outfit/hair and makeup too.

I mentioned before that a derby player may have different personas or alter egos on track and this is the perfect time to shine on game day, because while yes you have come to skate the audience has come to see you crash and jump and do crazy feats of wonder on skates.

It reminds me of the Colosseum, a great spectacular of a rather brutal unfolding of events of athleticism and well survival too. 100% injury risk, don't forget.

But ok you have donned your outfit, put together possibly a plate of food or baked goods for the food stall, attempted to eat something but also may be too nervous to stomach much (do try to fuel the body, it will need it) you will arrive at the venue with plenty of time to help lay the track if needed (volunteering is a huge component of Derby)

Don't forget to also join in on the team superstitions, travel together, meet for a meal, wear certain socks, eat the carbs before the game you will need the energy.

Do the team warm up, get your derby brain focused by any means possible because believe me when I say the chaos and confusion of a derby game needs focus, awareness and the ability to hold at least up to 3 different areas of focus.

What the refs are calling, where is the pack, where is the jammer, what is your bench coach screaming at you?

Who has lead?

Are you currently still on all 8 wheels, are you blocking in the right direction, did you have a plan going into this jam?

Have you thought at least 1 step ahead?

 ROLLERDERBY-The most ridiculously glorious game ever made

Did you stay in the track line?

I didn't feel the track rope

These are just a few of the things skater athletes that play derby will consider, sounds like most sports right?

Well yes of course, but don't forget, you still on roller skates, are we rolling right?

Am I balanced am I solid in my skates, if I'm gonna collide or make an obstacle have I sprawled or am I as small as I can be?

But that's the mental head space of game day,

how are you feeling physically? Did you get enough sleep?

Emotionally?
What is happening in your life and is it going to impact your game play?
Can you use the emotions to generate the required energy for the game?

Spiritually? Meditate, pray, listen to the right playlist, mantra, quote whatever the ritual might be give yourself enough time to get into that feeling.

But getting back to the mostly physically, you are about to put your body through an hour of pain, 2 x 30 minute intervals.

2 minute jams, 30 seconds between jams, breath, rest when you can, have several bottles of water ready, have a sweat cloth ready, when you are sitting at your bench do not pay attention to what is happening on track, do not think of any mistakes you have just made.

Instead focus on what you plan to do when you get your next 2 minutes.

Check in on the team mates, how are they, do you have a team plan?

Does your bench coach have some words to focus on?

You are still playing even while sitting on the bench.

If you do steal a glance to the scoreboard or to whats happening on the track be sure you've already prepared and have a few moments to appreciate and cheer your team but give yourself a good 20 seconds before the whistle blows to really reset your focus and the next 2 minutes.

And finally, the most important part of game day, that is above and beyond all game play, strategy, skating skills, game day jitters, all the skatey things that make this sport the best, and if you get nothing from the game but this, is please, whatever else you do, do not forget

You are here TO HAVE FUN !!!!!!!!!!!!

They made you a Jammer!

Oh SHIT!

Every position in derby has a particular intensity and purpose.

No one gets out of a jam without some kind of impact or fall... don't fear the fall... fear the fatigue instead...the eventual inability to get back up...

The first few jams the adrenaline has kicked into overdrive and you are ready to smash through walls and you feel like you could take on everyone and its awesome... don't get cocky...and don't waste your energy, conserve it.

Alternatively you can take a deep breath and just grind through pain for 2 minutes every jam, but seriously, your endurance and fitness better be on par if you choose that route.

You can work on a wall, hoping that they will fatigue eventually, you can roll side to side hoping to create gaps or open a lane that will get you through, there are options

You can sporadically have bursts of dynamic energy when timed right to get through a pack, the idea is to always know what your next step is going to be.

As a jammer you want to be dynamic as well as fluid, as well as fast and agile and well....its good to have all the skills as a jammer to keep the opposing team guessing what you will do next.

The jammer needs to rely both on the team and own capabilities, to get them through a pack and into lead jammer position.

From my own perspective jamming has a slightly different type of mindset to blocking, when I jam I am not thinking of making an impact but instead being effective while I move on the track, being adaptive and altering my movement as needed; where in blocking Im bracing for that impact while also trying to counteract the fast and often fancy footwork of Jammy skaters master Jedi abilities.

Block this

Blockers are the best... :)

they will stop all things on their track..

make you beg for mercy as they suck the life and soul out of you (leave the soul off track jammer) then you will have to yeild to them and be recycled like a piece of plastic. Repeat this cycle until more blockers come to save you and crush the wall in front of you, hooray!!

blockers use their bodies in such amazing ways, I have put my body, as a blocker, deliberately in the path of an oncoming big hit with the only thought being "brace for impact" I have the photo footage of me about to do just that and go flying. (please note the fact that my wheels are off the ground, Sophiopath is amazing! Also the resulting bruise of that landing!! EPIC!)

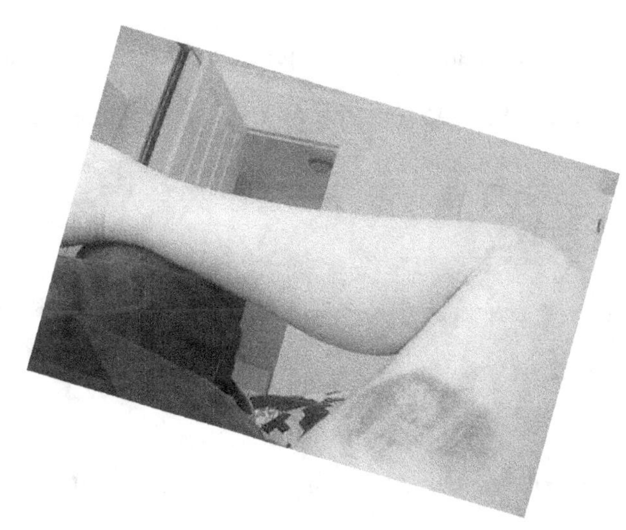

PIVOT

The pivot is both a blocker and potential Jammer, the pivot must be ready to do exactly that, go from playing one position and then pivoting into another.

The pivot can become the jammer if the current jammer hands them the star helmet cover.

Generally this only happens when the jammer has become overly stuck or lost lead jam and is getting no where.

The timing of cover or star pass (panty pass) is crucial, it can be an effective strategy or it can go horribly wrong depending on the timing.

The pivot is also often the jammer offense or an extra blocker the pivot moves much like a jammer but is effectively wanting to keep that star on the jammers head rather than theirs.

Laps

I have given laps its own section purely on the mental anguish this "basic" min skill has tormented me with from my very first attempt.

The skill is to do 27 laps in 5 minutes (while the rule book has adapted this to not be a requirement to play any more, its the principle of the matter to me now) this particular skill is my nemesis and also creates panic and anxiety within me to the point that after I finish it, most times, it results in vomiting.

My derby name is MuFasta and this is humorous because I really do need to move faster.

Doing laps I started out with 13

it soon proceeded to 16, 18,19, 21, 23, 23, 23, 23, 23……..lets say it was a frustrating 23 for a while.

25 was so bloody exciting, I was on a skater high for ages and almost 2.5 years later I got in my first 27!!!!!

Once I had finally done it the once, I was ok with never doing it again in my life time and I haven't so far, I could/should probably test myself again soon but now that goal was reached I am hoping that I don't attach so much angst to doing it again.

Release the kraken (stress)

As I write this chapter I'm listening to "voices in my head" by Nerdout and it just resonates with what I want to write about here.

Often women's anger (my own really), mental load or stress levels are labelled as overly emotional or sometimes even psychotic, a lot of the time (and I am generalising here) that anger has come about after a build up of repression of these particular emotions.

In a society that is currently experiencing escalating numbers in mental health, in particular depression and anxiety, roller derby is a particularly cool avenue for assisting with a type of recovery for mental health.

We know already, that exercise plays a really vital part in promoting positive mental health along with sports in general, but roller Derby is a little different in its approach.

I know that at Sunday training when someone comments on wanting "to hit things" I get a kind of a devilish smile knowing this is gonna be a great training session, it is also often me that is itching to 'hit' my friends.

I know this sounds a little strange, but when the focus is on skating, breaking through or pushing on walls getting a new skill or strategy it relieves the tension and stress of the week.

I have a high pressured management position and am a single parent of 3 wild alien children, 1 of whom is currently navigating that teenage stage.

Knowing that I have a space to let go of all of that for a little while, where others welcome the aggression, cheer it on in fact, is just so refreshing. 'They' (my teammates) will say to "hit harder, push harder, get lower, move faster".

All the while pushing back, hitting back.

It is a great tool and sport for Anger Management

If you ever find yourself angry at the world, angry at life, at people, at yourself, it doesn't matter who or what the anger is about, roller derby is the perfect outlet to transmute that anger into laser focused sportsmanship and athleticism.

Derby requires a level of mind, body, space, track and game awareness that I have never encountered before.

Often people say it just looks like a big cluster fuck of chaotic mess (which it does) but the strategy that is actually happening reminds me of the game of chess.

In that in derby you are playing both offensive and defensive and there are definitely sacrificial pawns, protect the Jammer (king) and the thinking 5 steps ahead, but don't forget...... this is all happening on wheels.

Releasing your potential

I mentioned the aha moment before (my coach loves witnessing aha moments), what I meant by that, is you first enter the world of skating thinking you have an idea on what it will be like (think flashback 80s skate rink vibes) and you fumble putting on your gear, yes even put it upside down or backwards and most definitely put on your wrist gaurds first before your skates that first time and than realise the error.

All of which may or may not fit properly, be uncomfortable, itchy and you feel awkward and clunky and of course you're now also on wheels.

You stand up for the first time on skates, or for the first time in years and you wobble, its not a natural feeling, seriously we were not designed on wheels, you have to develop the skills.

You roll around awkwardly hoping not to fall over, or you may glide smoothly if the muscle memory has been good to you.

Either way, roller derby is not just about roller skating, while yes it helps initially, it can be quite humbling and maybe a hit to the ego if you cant do some of the things you are being shown.

There comes a point where you become frustrated, but also hungry to improve and this is the space you want to always be reaching for, a roller derby skater is never done learning, never done pushing further.

Much like other sports, you can reach a level of expertise and effectiveness, even become elite.

However, you will always come up against an obstacle or a limit, it is here, where you get to realise your potential, you get to figure out how you are going to get past this perceived limitation and progress past it.

No holding back

I know that when I first started I was terrified, scared of falling, of injuring myself, of embarrassing myself, looking ridiculous, were others watching me?

I soon realised that nope everyone was pretty much in the same boat and the only people that were watching me were the coaches to make sure I was doing the things with as much safety as I could muster at the time.

I was holding back with everything, all of it, I was shy and timid and while I wasn't too bad on skates, I was definitely not going to play THE Derby, that was just out of scope of reality but it didn't take long to change my perspective.

To let go of the fear, no, the fear is still there, its feeling the fear but not letting it hold me back from doing the thing.

And there are LOT of things in roller derby to consider and holding back was simply doing that, holding me back.

Fears are natural, and for any athlete while yes, the body will be put through stress and you will feel exhausted, the mental mindset is just as (if not more so) important to consider in roller derby (all sports really).

You may not only have physical barriers creating obstacles but the psychological fears can be even more crippling.

I don't say this to scare anyone, but more to acknowledge the patterns involved in becoming a Roller Derby Athlete.

Often athletes will compare or measure their success based on their teammates or other teams and this only leads to a self intimidation that is both painful and unnecessary.

Understanding balance, momentum and gravity

Often at a skate fit session when learning to balance on one foot, glide or transition slowly from one foot to another, my hands in the prayer position, I practise Tai chi movements on skates to attempt to get some semblance of balance and coordination.

Often I am laughed at, and it I admit it is pretty funny to watch but I've found that the breathing, holding my core, the movement of the whole body while on skates creates all kinds of different motion and movement with my skates.

I let people know that its like wanting to have the skates not just be attached to my feet but be an extension of my body and it creates more awareness and confidence in skates.
I wear the skates, they do not wear me.

Gearing up

Safety is SEXY!!

Others will laugh at the amount of safety gear roller derby people wear, and think its not necessary, Ha!
I don't know how many times my helmet has saved me from head injuries or concussions and my knees, I would be in a wheelchair by now if not for my knee pads.

The gear for me is like armour, its me gearing up for war (a tad melodramatic maybe but it works as a great visual to get me in the right head space to play this full bodied contact sport, if you want a comparison think Tony Starks Iron man suit attaching to him style.

I mentally play out the close up of the gear, the music and effects in the background, preparing for battle, it works. Helmet first, there has been at least 2 occasions where i have had a concussion which would have been a lot worse if not having worn a helmet.

Knees – knee slides, four point falls, taking a knee for stability

Wrist gaurds – because basic instinct insists you put your hands out to save/catch your fall "barbie hands ya'll"or its broken fingers for you.

elbow pads– anywhere there's joints really is good to cover, when landing from a particularly hard hit, side swipe, wipe out or what i call "a Trace hit"

With an audience, it demands attention and a knowing that some awesome action is about to roll out

Inspiration

Much in line with motivation, roller derby brings with it such a myriad of ideas and awesomeness, I do believe that the world issues could be resolved on a road trip with derby people (read road trip chapter).

Its inspiring how much talent are among the derby folk.

You can find inspiration in so many places but to start with, roller derby incorporates, music, books (comics), movies, characters, people in your local communities, celebrities, quotes and puns, pictures, images and play on words.

It doesn't have to be logical to anyone but you, in derby, inspiration has to resonate with you, others don't need to understand what inspires you, but if it is a person, please let them know you are inspired by them.

I promise, the other person will be over the moon to hear that.

I know because I have had 2 people tell me this year that I have inspired them, and I seriously wanted to cry in appreciation at such a compliment.

I smiled and was blown away, (I don't think crying would have been quite understood but I couldn't believe they said it to me)

In derby you are able to inspire others simply by keeping going, by not giving up, that was something I had also never felt before, it was overwhelmingly heart warming.

I tell this story not to big note myself, instead I hope to convey that inspiration can come from outside but you can also be your own inspiration.

When you achieve something you never have, and suddenly you do start to truly believe that you can make changes to your life and perception of self, magic happens; and the universe scrambles to not only work with you but to then try to keep up.

Roller Derby gives you space to surpass your limits

You never know your limits, until you find yourself hitting one. This is where the hard part comes in… whether it is a physical barrier or mental block the frustration of reaching a limit repeatedly can become incredibly challenging.

I saw this great video that explained that even as much as pain as you are in when it comes to reaching a limit, your mind and body can achieve at least 40% more than you think when you have reached that barrier…

I often repeat in my head 40% when I want to stop or I think I've reached a limit.

Limits often require a level of of being able to sit in your discomfort, it is hard if you are fearful or have doubts; but allowing yourself the time to stay in this discomfort long enough to build the capacity to overcome the limit is a greatness that feels amazing to accomplish.

Your desire and motivation play a key role in surpassing limits and roller derby does this (if you let it) for every session you will get out of it what you put in, like all sports its the willingness to feel or look ridiculous in order to overcome the uncertainties or insecurities to achieve the physical capabilities.

The language you use, Phrases like "I can't," or "I'm too tired, too sore," are words that will limit you, if you have difficulty with using these word rephrase them slightly. "I cant, becomes " I cant yet" I m too tired becomes "I'm here and I'm working" I'm too sore" becomes "this is building my strength, this will get me where I need to go"

Consistency in habit is so important for overcoming limits, deciding to make the commitment to be open to the idea of exploring your limits, to face the challenge of surpassing them will be one of the most satisfying feelings you will ever experience.

Surpassing limits to success takes focus and awareness of self.

That when training in roller derby, know the difference between training and gameplay, being humble and being fiercely competitive in the real game play.

Focus on specific areas, foundations, certain skills, working through the motions, when tired, or sore and being able to find the energy.
Looking for the small progressions, counting the clock of how many more times the whistle is going to blow, how many laps can you do? How much more can you push, how much can you give and take?

The pay off of surpassing limits can be both exhilarating as well as daunting, because when you reach a perceived limit you come to the understanding that you could be so much more, aim for so much more, limits suddenly become limitless and you wonder why you didn't think or know of this before.

But its simple, you hadn't lived it yet, hadn't seen within yourself that it can be done, but now you know, it can, go get it and get at it.

Trust and confidence is a must in roller derby and this can take time; if these qualities are not naturally present, have faith in knowing they can be developed.

As you learn each skill, you can start to have trust in yourself and your team to be where you need to be. You can be confident in the knowing that you have practised this again and again and that is how limits are overcome.

Try not to compare yourself to other skaters, ever, each skater is uniquely different; and while general skate skills will crossover the way each persons body moves is also just too different to compare.

So limits to overcome will look different to the individual, and never doubt for a minute that even the elite derby player has a limit they are looking to surpass, I promise.

speed

"you look like you want to go faster Nikki"

I was working on skating backwards (my all time favourite skatey skill) and I was struggling to build momentum I would shuffle around a bit like a bambi but it was the coach who came up (the same coach who got me falling by the way) and said, "trust me, I will steer you, just hold on, get low and we're going to go faster, you look like you want to go faster Nikki, how about it?"

"ok, sure I'll have a go"

Suddenly I was flying, it wasn't even that fast (I can go so much faster now) but it was exhilarating.

In that moment I was in what I dub "my happy place" I had on the biggest goofiest grin, and my heart was racing and the adrenaline hit and I was as free as what I flying feels like (skydiving is a close second).

Its so hard to describe this feeling with the right words that express the sheer joy I felt in that moment, I don't think I had ever felt so alive.

I didn't know whether to laugh, cry, scream or just hang on for dear life, my face said it all, the sheer awesomeness that I just got to experience was written all over it.

I was hooked

Freedom

Skating for me became the place I could DE-load the mental clutter, nothing else has ever come close (perhaps once dance did a similar thing) to this feeling of freedom and flying to where the world would just disappear and experience was all that was needed, thoughts would leave my mind and I was purely in my body and just feeling the experience.

Skating for me is an escape from adult hood, from responsibilities from being a single mum with 3 kids, a manager, expectations and roles wash away and I get to be a free spirit in that moment.

I would describe it much like a spirit monk would experience enlightenment or the euphoria of faith or answered prayer for religious folk, that may be the best comparison, skating to me, feels like nourishment for the soul.

It feels like home.

you get A pack " the pack is here"

So " the Pack" in derby is where the majority of players are in an upright position within the engagement zone, or something like that (google the rule people, derby is confusing).

But the pack is also what your team becomes, the best thing about this team sport is that you are never alone, there is always someone to talk to or talking to you (or yelling to get your attention) whether it be a teammate the bench, coach a ref, the audience, the first advise I was given when I played my first game was to find my team, or find a friend and stick with them.

"find the friendly side" when jamming and you are coming up to a pack or a wall yes, you can impact at full speed if you know the opponents and that you can overcome that, however, if you are unsure or hesitant its effective to wash off the speed and look for the friendly side, use your own team to propel you, whip you around the track, look for elbows and hips of the same colour and let them push you, they are your team never fear them. Don't get in their way but let them help however they can.

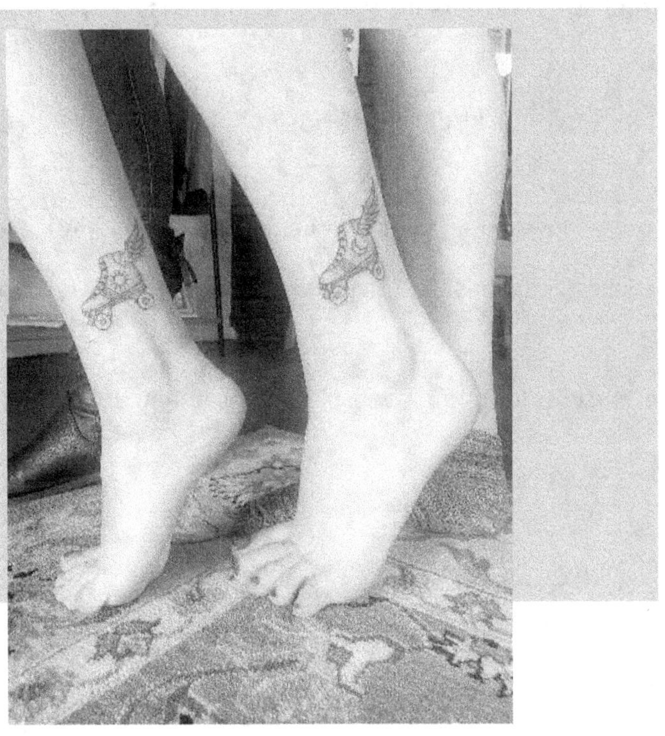

identity

The term being a 'derby girl' is unique to each person (though is a little outdated with the gendered title, but still a piece of cultural history "derby peep", "athletes", "skatey frenz" or "roller folk" are great alternatives) but the term also has some generalised stigmas attached as well.

'Derby girls' have grit, and attitude, they're not afraid to scrape their knee or get a bruise or 5 when it means they have battle wounds to display.

A derby or 'roller girl' will be witty or sarcastic, often passionate about a cause that they are an avid activist about.

Intelligence and cleverness are usual along with charisma.

Not to mention, generally Athletic (perhaps not at first but eventually it becomes a part of the identity).

'Derby girls' do to the things that make them sporty, often have a DIY spirit in which they design their own uniforms/costumes, Frankenstein their skates and utilise the resources at their disposal.

Interestingly, most 'roller girls' have a very independent streak and a self reliance that is borderline obsessive.

Confident is the roller girl, assertive and often a leader in other areas of their community (the confidence also may not be present at first, but again, its an eventuality of the aggression that comes with playing the Derby, inevitably women soon learn that taking hits or overcoming an obstacle is no deterrent both on the track and in life).

The urban dictionary describes the roller girl as "commonly described as living Wonder Women" and this is a perfect analogy.

The best way to describe the roller derby identity is "a head turner"
An experience I recently had, was that I was with my team and we were heading out to a drag show and we all were dressed up.
The fashion amoungst it was a little phenomenal, we entered the venue as a group and between the vintage look, goth look, buisiness look, sparkles, makeup, and just pure EXTRA- ness all heads turned and stared, people just stared, it was movie montage worthy of a Charlie's angel's hair flick and pose or slo-mo to freeze frame.

Because we cause impact, especially in a group, its hard not to notice, and also to be both admiring of and intimidated by.
I know that when I first saw it, I stared too; and then there was a longing feeling to be a part of that..... walking into an event with such people makes me stand taller, and again that inner smile of just knowing how awesome we are spreads over me and I feel amazing.

I don't speak of this to sound arrogant or egotistical around the aesthetics of people, I speak of the presence of people, the energy they exude, derby folk have a great presence about them; and when in a group, whether on or off skates, the charismatic energy produced is impressive.

Strength

People often ask me, is derby rough?
Well yeah, it is.

I think it surprises a lot of people just how fit and healthy and strong you need to be to play roller derby.

Its part of a realisation process.

That knowing how to roller skate is not going to be enough to play the sport, but as I mentioned earlier this unique sport is a brilliant positive mental health builder.

It is this because it gives space to face fears; and challenges; and then overcome them to build resistance.

It teaches relationship building and camaraderie of a team; it gives community and social engagement.

It promotes healthier lifestyles; and it is simply, fun.

When I speak of strength I believe it is both improving mindset along with the developing the physical body, it is both (always both).

Strength comes in many forms, what roller derby does, is give you the feeling of being strong, brave, fearless while also being vulnerable enough to look ridiculous at the same time (you are on wheels remember) there is always the chance you will fall over.

But, I have to admit, that moment, when you land a jump, take a hit, get through a wall or learn that new skill; and you are upright and remaining standing strong in your skates; you feel invincible in that moment; and it is a great experience.

Awesome people

I am yet to meet a person that skates that isn't awesome in all different kinds of ways, the skaters I roll with are nurses, doctors, musicians, artists, awesome individuals from all walks of life.

But what I have noticed primarily is that each individual has some pretty strong core beliefs and values and almost always have a cause.

In the few years alone that I have been skating, I have never been a part of so many fundraisers, cultural awareness raising and just plain more awareness of the happenings in our world and just how many humans are supporting each other through some great challenges this world is facing.

Physical health and fitness, well-being, Mental health supports and awareness, sexual identity, homelessness, youth support, domestic violence, to name just a few areas that have weaved through roller derby that our league and team have contributed to, building awareness and education or raising funds to support local ideas.

we skate, because running sux

My awesome teammate made these awesomely fabulous tie-dyed shirts with the quote "We skate because running sux" and of course for me it was a very truthful statement, moreover, I sucked at running. But here's the kicker, skating gave me the confidence to learn to run and then my new goal ended up being "I want to run, on skates" this weird quirky obsession of mine really changed my perspective on how to see exercise and what I could do with my body.

Where previously I would avoid anything that would cause pain to my body, or would give up if I couldn't complete a skill.

I now love the challenge, I have bought like 20 sweat headbands with the absolute clarity that I will be sweating out my eyeballs on the daily, it was a solid investment.

Exercise can become addicting, soon you will be reminding yourself that you need to rest more than you need to do something active, that is the power of intrinsic motivation towards exercise.

You want the soreness and when you start to see the results it steels your determination and mental will power further and it becomes an amazing experience, as your energy levels improve and you generally just feel better physically and mentally.

For the Skater

Roller derby is designed by the skater, for the skater, every aspect of the game has been designed by volunteer skaters who just want to continue to see this awesome sport evolve.

From literally building the track at the beginning of a skate event to the continuation of a league, getting people rolling, travelling time, money and effort of every member in a derby league.

Literal blood sweat and tears are common finds on the derby track, people volunteer their time for putting together coaching sessions, games, events, continual skate programs, marketing and social media honestly, like I said before, committees of derby leagues should be in politics, they would have the world sorted in the 9-5 and still be home in time to run the household and then go skating.

The community is amazing.

Learning the Rules for life

Derby has a LOT of rules, all put in place for your safety and to keep each other from causing harm or injury.

There is a manual/book of rules along with online tests to quiz your knowledge of all the derby things, its extensive and often overly complicated, much like the rules for life, derby is both incredibly complex and yet so simple in its entirety.

I have found a way to incorporate or even often compare roller derby around most/to all aspects of my life, it may seem like an unhealthy obsession to others, but from this one sport I can see so many comparable life patterns, its quite ridiculous, gloriously so.

I have become a better individual and overall human being because of this sport.

It has taught me so many things I cant even begin to explain (although this book is an attempt I suppose)

Roller derby brings me to life, I see it in others too, and now I see it in other places too.

When someone loves something and their whole body radiates outwards and you cant help but smile, that is what roller derby does to me it brings me to life...

one coach I had summed it up perfectly, she said

"I Love it how derby relates to real life in so many ways. If you fall down get back up, you can do anything for 2 minutes, and wear protective gear always....also don't be a dick to the people who's job it is to keep you safe just say yes thank you reff and go about your day."

I can bring back (annoyingly so) any conversation to derby.

Equally Physically and mentally intense,

I have written briefly already about the positive mental health and physicality of roller derby however, its worth diving a little deeper into the how's of the sport.

Roller Derby is high on impact on the body, as a full body contact sport, yes people are going to make contact with you; and yes you are going to fatigue and fall.

Often.

You will become unbalanced, lose your footing, stumble, trip over nothing (its the derby ghosts, I swear), be physically pushed to exhaustion.

A conversation I hear often is that skaters are surprised at how fit you really need to be to play the sport well.

Not only is it physically taxing you also have the mental aspects of this game.

It is not gentle on the mind.

There is strategy and track awareness needed, you will become frustrated when learning a new skill or drill and you will become frustrated as you improve because new goals will form.

If you are injured (100% injury risk sport) recovery can also be taxing.

There is also the element that you are attempting to accomplish several things at once.

You are working as a team, checking on the other team, listening for the bench coach, the reffs, and don't forget, your still on skates!

Are your feet where they are supposed to be?

remember that everyone else is on skates too... at any moment another player can become an obstacle or trip hazard as well and you don't want to find yourself as part of a track collision pile up.

Trust Building in its weirdest form

Becoming a part of the team

Watching how a team is built in this sport is fascinating, my league naturally just folds in new players, (myself included) through a bridging program from skate fit (learning how to skate) through to game play, I wasn't even aware until about a year later when I found myself saying to a new skater, hey no you're doing amazing and you've got this (it made me want to laugh and cry in that moment) that I realised I was a part of something extraordinary and exceptional, I'd become a part of the power of the team.

Understanding the new skaters story is where I always start.

I ask the question, what brought you to skating?

What about it called you?

I have a firm belief that skating will find you when you need it, there will be a call to take action, generally a person is looking for something fun, but also a way to do exercise that doesn't feel like exercise and skating is a skill you can pick up at any point in your life, from childhood right though to being an elder (elder athlete here).

The diversity of the 'why' is always so fascinating,

"I'm here to have me time"

"I want to do something for myself"

"I needed to do something, but I hate the gym"

"I loved skating as a kid at the local rink"

"Skating looks fun"

And…. The list goes on, I had no idea that when I put on skates that I would want to become a derby player.
Sure I liked the idea of it, but I was pretty realistic in my expectations of what I could do on skates.
It took time and a heck of a lot of encouragement to continue to play this ridiculously glorious game.

Bouncing back from Injury

Full bodied contact sport, 100% injury risk, it is not a matter of if, but rather, when.
I have seen broken wrists, ACL's.
I have seen sprains and bruises on all parts of the body.

Believe it or not I am actually a pacifist, I believe violence is never an answer towards any person. In saying that, I have been responsible for various damage caused in this sport, I have nail gauged and bruised others, even to go so far as to give someone a black eye (not deliberately).

My own experience has seen bruised legs, wrist, thumbs (fingers rolled over, good lesson to not leave your hand on the ground after a fall, butt and hip bruises, and yep I even once sat on my skate during a fall and had a bruise where one should never be bruised (except in pleasure) way too painful.

I have had a sprained wrist, ankle and have also broken my left ankle bone in 2 places.

I have woken up the next day after a training session or after a game and been so sore I could barely walk or move.

I don't say any of this to scare people away, no, the opposite actually, its a sport that requires a significant amount of resilience and endurance.

If you are looking for a healthy way to become strong both mentally and physically this is a challenge well worth picking up.

Its a raw, real sport and its a type of contact that generally (as I spoke briefly on previously) that is not often seen or smiled upon in a primary female-gendered stereotype.

Injury is a natural part of this sport, however, every skater responds to injury differently.

Some want to be left alone to heal without any interaction from their team but some well wishing and that's all. Others need more reassurance that they are still very much a part of the community and welcome to come back and be a part of it whenever they want.

For example, when I broke my ankle, I still went to as many training sessions as possible and took photos and posted on our social media page all the amazing things the team was doing, I NSO'd at the local scrim, I took notes, I researched team building activities.

Sometimes these distractions helped, I learnt plenty from watching, but also don't mistake my love and enthusiasm for the sport with my ability to overcome the mental and physical health issues that would present themselves along with the injury.

While I was contributing in a different way, I also felt annoyed and angry that I couldn't be skating. That others looked at me with pity and I looked at them with longing, it wasn't an easy pill to swallow.

I focused on what I could do every day with the smallest of progressions and I made sure to follow the doctors and physio's orders to the letter.

I was incredibly determined to get back on skates. But I could also see quite easily how easy it would be to give up and just not go back, too.

The thought was there, the crazy, ridiculous mind fuck that you don't realise will hit you, until it does.

The first time I put my skates back on after the break, I cried, and then I had a panic attack and then it took me a little while to pull myself together and then it felt, clunky, awkward, I couldn't do basic skills right, I didn't move right and my ankle just plain hurt.

Of course, as I describe this, I eye roll at myself, for many people have been through worse injury than me and have bounced back or made the comeback even stronger.

I really had nothing to complain about, it didn't stop the fact that as a single parent of 3 active kids with a full time job, I had other responsibilities to consider on top of being injured, and while I could mostly put on a brave face and a smile for my friends, family and kids; it didn't stop the tears from falling when I finally got myself into the shower after a long day of hobbling about.

It sucked.

I wont lie, but then I also have some great people in the derby community who have also had injuries, and I looked to them a lot.

That if they could be injured and come back to skate again, so could I and god dangit my mid life crisis and new found life goal/dream of being an elder athlete was not to be shelved just yet.

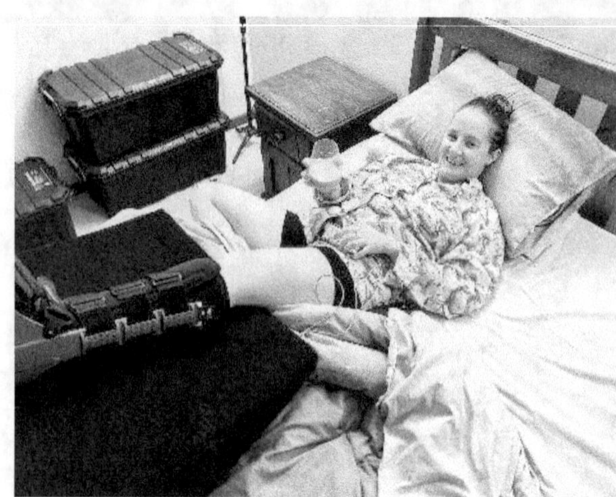

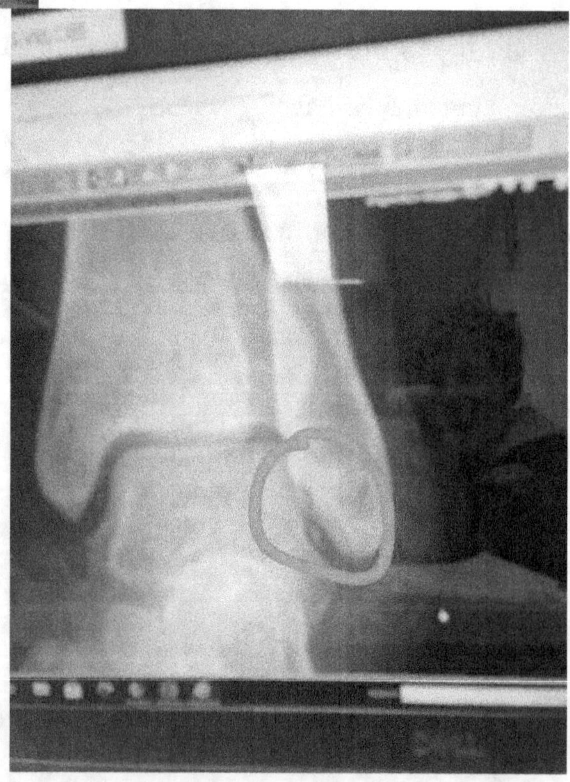

Because this dream had been enbedded in me for years, let me tell you the tale of how my dream of being an elder athlete came to be.......

Six months into my learning to skate, I got to go to Derbyfest which is a 3-4 day skate festival for non stop roller derby madness.

Its brilliant.

You get to be coached by elite players in workshops and you get to watch elite level games that are just phenomenal as you watch the Olympic skate gods do their thing on wheels.

In saying all that, I had my first mental and emotional meltdown at this first Derby Fest where I realised that 6 months on skates had not prepared me at all for the level of athleticism I was witnessing being performed on skates and the realisation of how crap I really am and just how much more I had to learn was not only overwhelming but incredibly disheartening.

I was a mid 30 year old woman learning roller derby, what planet did I think I was living on where that was a realistic notion?

I had the realisation that in order for me to play a normal game of derby, I would have to become an athlete, I would have to work on my body more than I ever had before (and I was a dancer who previously did ballet 6 days a week, my body was well associated with pain) but I honestly in that moment felt my soul be crushed a little at a lost dream.

I remember sitting in a line waiting to do a workshop with a team mate, she just knew and straight up asked "are you OK?"

I felt the tears and the emotions coming and I couldn't stop them and I said out loud "i shouldn't be here, I am never going to play a game of Roller derby, I feel stupid" and it was heart wrenching, the inner child in me was silently crying too (even now, years later, as I write this story I get emotional, because its still a raw feeling of letting go of something that I truly loved) but what my team mate said to me that day will remain with me long after I hang up my skates) she said

"Nikki, how long have you been skating?"

I replied six months.

She said, "right so thats what? 2 sessions of skatefit? Yeah- 24 weeks of an hour program and what maybe 10 weeks of training, that's like about 50-60 hours tops – that's no more than 3 days of actual skating, in fact, you will have skated more in these 3 days than you have in the last 6 months.

You're here, doing the skating, those other people, the elite skaters, have been skating for years, some of them decades.

You just need more time on your skates. And we can get you there, trust the team to get you there, give us one year to get you there and *you will* play a game of roller derby.

Her belief in me in that moment was extraordinary, I didn't have that belief in myself at all, I was giving up, but here was this person that wasn't going to let me just walk away, I hope she knows (I hope I've told her often enough) just how amazing that is and how much this world needs more of her magic.

Because I played my first game of roller derby less then 6 months after that.

I tell this story to let people know that its ok to have defeatist moments, that sometimes dreams die but others are conjured and I also tell this story to acknowledge that I couldn't do this on my own.

I needed the help, and that having teammates, who truly believe in you, when you don't have the strength to believe in yourself, is one of the greatest gifts I've ever had the privilege of being given.

Trauma and therapy healing

Living in such an unstable time as the 2020 global pandemic (words I use too often now) is not something any of us thought or expected to be facing, and as wave after wave of uncertainty and fear surrounding the virus has really left an impact on a global level that we can not possibly comprehend the aftermath in years to come of this event.

Often in Derby (primarily women) are seeking a safe space to build strength to overcome some form of trauma, whether they are aware of this or not makes no difference, it is easy to identify if you know to look for it.

And while I would never speak of it to them as directly as I have written it here, I acknowledge I don't know a person's story until they want to share that part of themselves, or they may never choose to do so and both are accepted in Derby.

Sometimes words don't do a thing and having such a tactile sport to express some of the repression is all for the good.

The visceral experience gives space to overcome the thoughts or thinking process.

A lot of the time skaters will come to Derby and need reassurance to overcome a variety of anxieties, thoughts often associated with shame, body imaging and self deprecation (I am no exception to this rule) every skater I have ever had the privilege of skating with has voiced the very fear of not being good enough, or become frustrated with themselves and what their bodies will and wont do.

I don't say this as a generalisation, I'm stating a fact.

The good news though in all this is that skaters will receive the benefits of a community that will reassure them that they are, and have always been, more than enough and now, that a skater can start to recognise that, we together can overcome and recover from any limit or obstacle in eventuality.

Gritty and grit teaching resilience

I have said many times already that derby is not a gentle sport, I reiterate that because people for some reason don't believe me when I say that, new skater, you are now an athlete, you don't just put on a pair of wheels and dive into roller derby (sorry) no, you have to do all the skatey things and learn the skate skills that will get you there.

And you will not learn by watching, reading a book or watching Youtube, you will have to put on the skates, a lot and you will have to look foolish a lot, and fall over a lot and repeat movements over and over, a lot.
Derby teaches a kind of self discipline that lets a person grow and develop, it teaches how to remain calm in the chaos and how to communicate with others.

Courage after the hit

In Derby, much like life, you will get knocked down.

The best thing you learn in derby is how to get back up after the hit.

Every now and then though the hit may be bigger or harder than expected and you go down and suddenly, you're shaken, intimidated, a person has side swiped you and sent you flying and for a moment your life flashes before your eyes and you know you are going to crash the landing.

You are down, you are winded possibly broken somewhere and you pause for that second to let your brain catch up with what your body has just experienced.

I must say again, nothing about this sport is normal, and none of your reactions are to be embarrassed by (high pitched girly squeal and manic hysterical laughter person right here).

I've watched a skater come barrelling down the straight of the track and I have both headed in to brace for the hit but also stepped out of the way of the freight train knowing that if I hit that I would end up broken.

Self preservation is definitely a natural response "fight or flight" can remain intact thank you very much.

The mindset of this game is important to establish before you even step foot or skate on a track.

Check your mindset before playing, check your body, are you warmed up enough, did you get good sleep, what have you eaten today?

Who are you playing with?

What is the vibe of the team?

Do you have any injuries and have you let your coach know?

The adrenaline hits pretty strong during a game because everything is happening so fast and that fight or flight kicks in and you can become overwhelmed at all the things happening at once.

Dont forget to Breathe, stay focused and if you do get hit and you are down allow yourself a moment to check everything is alright, especially if you have been pushed off track, take a moment to see what is happening on the track, take a look around and find the gap or the place you need to be that best supports the team.

This is where your courage steps in, it starts not being about the hits or the defence or offence – it becomes more about the flow of the team being reestablished.

Hitting back – there comes a time in roller derby where you have learnt that sometimes someone is going to hit you, you might fall down, or ricochet or just feel the impact and brace for the hit.

It becomes instinctive (survival right?) but at some point, maybe not straight away, but after a while, you are going to get annoyed at being hit all the time and there will come a moment when you realise, you are allowed to hit back.

That you don't have to just stand there and take the hit.

It actually took someone else telling me that I can hit back for me to even realise that.
It didn't register in my pacifist brain to even consider hitting a person with my body.

I feel embarrassed remembering the thought, was that really ok…in a world that usually states "its wrong to hit" to suddenly have the freedom to make contact with others … it takes getting used to.

At first my focus was just staying upright on my skates, and trying to get back up quickly.
But eventually I got lower, learnt to lean in to the hit or brace for the impact but also manouvre my body into the 'catch' position and the hit back.

In derby you can use your shoulders, your hips, your butt and the front of your body in general – think open backed hospital gowns as the 'go for impact' spots – nothing to be touched from the neck up, knees and elbows down or along the spine for obvious fatal injury areas.

That still leaves a whole lot of body surface area for the taking, and I've been winded, ribbed, had bruises along my arms and legs and hips and thighs I've landed on a skate (literally sat on my own skate in a fall) had others roll over my fingers, legs, land on me and other crazy wild happenings on a track.

I've lost my temper and gone for the big hits, attempted to jam around people, under people, over people, it gets wildly wacky with what bodies can do on skates.

There's a pattern in its brilliance

 Strategic growth and development – I mentioned earlier that derby is played both offensively and defensively, but this is not where the plays and strategies end.

Like chess derby is thought out moves ahead and if you don't have the track awareness and know where you need to be or have an idea of what your plan is, you will either get left standing in roller dust, will react impulsively instead and end up either in the sad place, or get caught in the cluster fuck of chaos resulting most likely with you on your ass, knees or flying. Many a time I find myself literally standing with my head moving side to side attempting to figure out what the heck is happening... Often it reminds me of a tennis match movement and must look ridiculous, but I often laugh at myself doing this. Roller Derby has a rhythm, a flow, it moves like a dance in some instances, and if you watch enough of the sport you start to see the patterns, the strategies unfolding, until the hit.

Volunteer

so you want to be apart of the derby verse but you have come to accept that there is one slight problem, you really can't skate and the thought of actually being on wheels does not appeal to you at all....

However you want to be a part of the awesomeness somehow.

Woo, we need you and want you dearly!!!!

Roller derby takes an immense amount of volunteer work, whether its laying track, commentating, putting together a playlist, doing peoples hair in cool viking braids, standing/sitting at an event door, cooking up a storm for a fund raising food stall, helping sell merchandise, yell scream and cheer on the sidelines, be a non skating official, be a benchy, a coach, a cheerleader, a mum who brings extra water bottles or bags of lollies.
Will help create content and market on social media, has a first aid certificate, is friends with a paramedic (no person is turned away, we have a job for you!) and every job or task helps make the magic of roller derby happen, without it the skaters could not do what they do.

Random Derby Quotes to live by that just need mentioning...

" Derby Stance, its like squashing a watermelon with your vagina"

"We're grown adults on roller skates, we already look fucking ridiculous"

" Turn on your Vag lights"

"I miss hitting my friends" I want to hit my friends

"you cant be unhappy on roller skates"

The first game, the last jam the first jam – I didn't die!!!!!

What else has derby taught me?

To be ALL IN, in other aspects of my life, as a mother, a manager, a leader, an athlete, in my friendships and relationships

The derby verse has no idea the impact it has had on my life and the lives of others, (it is the derby superpower) that the team/community lent me strength when I am sure I had none and I can only hope to pay that forward.

I wrote this book to express my love of the sport, but as I was writing I realised that it is the people and community that makes this sport truly exceptional.

To all the derby folk I have ever met and had the privilege to skate with or just hang out with and to all the skaters that follow.
I say thank you.
I love you and I can only hope, much like the jammers panty when I'm stuck in the sad place I hope to – PASS IT ON.
That is, pass on the super power and wisdoms, and awe inspiring examples that can be produced only by this most ridiculously glorious game ever made.

Reference and link to further derby rule confusion!

https://static.wftda.com/beginner-curriculum/This-is-Roller-Derby.pdf